Visitor's Guide to
THE LOIRE

D1258459

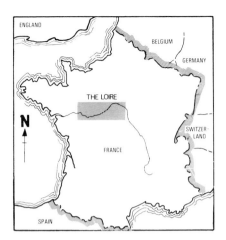

Visitor's Guide Series

This series of guide books gives, in each volume, the details and facts needed to make the most of a holiday in one of the tourist areas of Britain and Europe. Not only does the text describe the countryside, villages, and towns of each region, but there is also valuable information on where to go and what there is to see. Each book includes, where appropriate, stately homes, gardens and museums to visit, nature trails, archaeological sites, sporting events, steam railways, cycling, walking, sailing, fishing, country parks, useful addresses — everything to make your visit more worthwhile.

Other titles already published or planned include:

The Lake District (revised edition)
The Chilterns
The Cotswolds
North Wales
The Yorkshire Dales
Cornwall
Devon
East Anglia
Somerset and Dorset
Guernsey, Alderney and Sark
The Scottish Borders
    and Edinburgh
The Welsh Borders
Historic Places of Wales
The North York Moors, York and
    the Yorkshire Coast
Peak District (revised edition)
South and West Wales
Hampshire and the Isle of Wight
Kent
Sussex
Dordogne (France)
Brittany (France)
Black Forest (W Germany)
The South of France
Tyrol
French Coast
Iceland

KEY FOR MAPS

Towns - Villages

Motorways

Main Roads

Country Boundary

County Boundary

Rivers

Lakes/Reservoirs

Museum/Art Gallery/Centre

Archaeological Site

Building/ Country Park Gardens

Castle/Fort

Ecclesiastical Building

Wildlife Park/Zoo Nature Reserve

Other Place of Interest

The Visitor's Guide To
THE LOIRE

Norman Brangham

MOORLAND PUBLISHING

HUNTER
PUBLISHING INC

British Library Cataloguing in
Publication Data

Brangham, N.
    The visitor's guide to the Loire.
    1. Loire Valley (France) —
    Description and travel — Guide-
    books
    I. Title
    914.4′504838   DC611.L81

Published by
Moorland Publishing Co Ltd,
8 Station Street,
Ashbourne, Derbyshire,
DE6 1DE England.
Tel: (0335) 44486

ISBN 0 86190 134 7 (paperback)
ISBN 0 86190 135 5 (hardback)

Published in the USA by
Hunter Publishing Inc,
300 Raritan Center Parkway,
CN94, Edison, NJ 08818

ISBN 0 935161 43 0 (paperback)

Printed in the UK by
Butler and Tanner Ltd,
Frome, Somerset.

ACKNOWLEDGEMENTS

I am grateful for the factual help I have
received while preparing this book from:
Mrs Pauline Hallam, Director of Public
Relations, and her assistant, Miss Beatrice
Jeffries, at the French National Tourist Office
in London; Miss Caroline McCarthy, Press
Assistant at French Railways in London; the
Comité Régional de Tourisme, Nantes; finally,
my wife, many of whose observations noted
during our journeyings in the Loire Valley
have been included in the text.

Colour illustrations have been supplied by:
N. Brangham (Ussé); C.W. Footer (Chinon,
Chenonceau); H. Race (Chaumont, St
Aignan-sur-Cher); the remaining colour
illustrations and all the black-and-white
photographs have been supplied by the
French National Tourist Office Photo
Library and Mrs Florence Beddow.

Contents

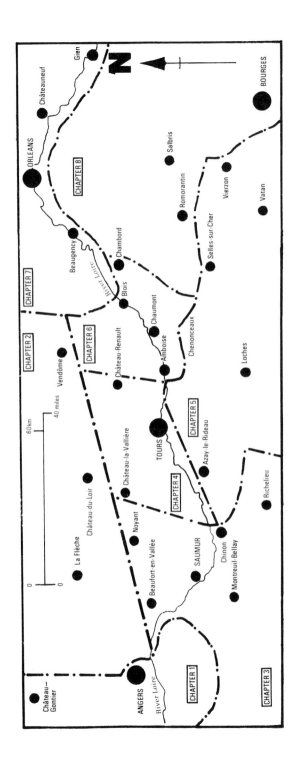

Introduction

The Region of the Loire Valley

Most guide books to regions of France can use ancient historical provinces to determine boundaries for them: Burgundy, Brittany or Provence, for instance. So habitual is it to refer to areas of France by their pre-Revolution provincial names that they seem to constitute natural, self-contained entities. The Loire Valley does not fall into this category. Its name is as familiar as any province — indeed, better known than many French provinces — yet it has never been a province. At one time or another small provinces and counties — Maine, Anjou, Touraine, Blois, Orléans and Berry — have sat astride what is conventionally understood as the Loire Valley. Anjou and Touraine are the only names still in common use; they take up the lion's share of the valley, but not all.

A tradition has grown up which has come to accept the Loire Valley as lying between Gien in the east and Angers in the west. In short, châteaux country. Châteaux have made the fame of this section of the river.

The French Revolution abolished the autonomy of the provinces and replaced them by *départements*. Below are the old provinces and the *départements* of today which correspond to them, and their administrative capitals. In brackets are the departmental numbers used in post-codes; they also identify the provenance of a car by the last two numbers on its registration plates.

Maine: Sarthe (72), Le Mans; Mayenne (53), Laval.
Anjou: Maine-et-Loire (49), Angers.
Touraine: Indre-et-Loire (37), Tours.

Orléanais: Loiret (45), Orléans; Eure-et-Loire (28), Chartres; Loir-et-Cher (41), Blois.
Berry: Cher (18), Bourges; Indre (36), Châteauroux.

Mayenne and Eure-et-Loire lie outside our region. When the *départements* were invented, the majority acquired their names from the main rivers flowing through their territory. With a plethora of rivers in the Loire Valley, the revolutionary politicians chose, it will be seen from the list I have just given, extraordinarily clumsy hyphenated names which the visitor has the utmost difficulty in memorising.

To add a little confusion, you will see on modern maps a region known as Val de Loire or Centre, and another called Western Loire or Pays de la Loire. Together, they spread over an amorphous area without organic reality; they are post-war politico-economic inventions with little relevance for the visitor.

If Gien and Angers are traditional and convenient markers of the east and west boundaries of the Loire Valley, what about north and south? There is no particular tradition here. So, for this book, the arbitrary northern limit of our bailiwick is a line drawn roughly from Château-Gontier through Vendôme to Orléans. To the south, I include Richelieu and Loches; the eastward projection of this line just squeezes in Bourges (not normally included in guides to the region).

Five Michelin maps (scale 1:200,000) cover the area: No 63 for a small part west of Angers; 64 for most of the rest;

63 for the district around Gien; 68 is just needed for the southerly part between Richelieu and Loches; 60 for Bourges.

Within this quadrilateral is a natural unity of geography, climate and culture. Within the unity is enough diversity for eye and mind to find constant fresh stimulus. The visitor who falls under the spell of this part of France will find that his curiosity carries him beyond the strict confines of this book so as to make his own discoveries.

It is time to place the Loire, as the main artery of our quadrilateral, in the context of the whole river. It rises out of a high plateau in Vivarais (Ardèche) just below the rounded hump of Mont Gerbier-de-Jonc. Its rivulet life begins at 1,400m and sets off briskly in a southerly direction through pasturelands to be diverted northwest at Rieutord by the massive Suc de Bauzon mountain, but for whose presence the Loire would have finished up in the Mediterranean. Instead, it passes through the cold and sparsely inhabited uplands of Auvergne (crossed by R.L. Stevenson at Goudet on his immortal donkey Modestine, as related in *Travels with a Donkey in the Cevennes*) to the dramatic volcanic site of Le Puy-en-Velay. Then it works its way through the Loire gorges to Roanne. Gradually the river opens out and slows its tempo as in its maturity it reaches the warmer and more hospitable lowlands. Comfortable, small riverside towns appear: Digoin, Dompierre, Decize, Nevers. Near the latter, the important tributary of the Allier joins the Loire. Thereafter, and all the way to Angers, other rivers flow into the Loire; from the south come Loiret, Cosson, Beuvron, Cher, Indre, Vienne, Thouet, Louet, Layon; from the northern side come Cisse, Authion, Loir, Mayenne, Maine and Sarthe.

After Nevers come the first famous wine names, Pouilly and Sancerre. At Gien, the now majestic river begins a great westward arc with Orléans at its most northerly point. This arc is a deflection by the harder rocks of the Beauce to the north during the Tertiary era when the upland mass of the Massif Central was being formed. Otherwise the Loire would have flowed into the Seine. At the same time, the land mass tilted very slightly westwards, and the Atlantic Ocean, rising many metres on account of melting ice caps flowed into western France as far as Touraine. Sologne, south of Orléans, was formed by the sandy detritus brought down by the Loire from the Massif Central. Innumerable meres (*étangs*), forest and heathland cover the Sologne flatlands, giving it a haunting atmosphere which is in marked contrast to the open countryside further west. Once an immense oak forest covered this acid soil and spread to the other side of the Loire to form the Forêt d'Orléans. Hunting, shooting and fishing are dominant activities.

In the Blésois and Touraine the Loire flows in a generally southwest direction through the broad valley once covered by the Atlantic when it was the Mer des Faluns. Layers of limestone rich in fossil deposits (*faluns*) were laid down. Later, over them, calcareous clay with sand and mica was sedimented, visible today as riverside chalk cliffs (*tuffeaux*) out of which were dug troglodyte caves. Sometimes whole villages were built in this way, their chimneys poking through the grass and trees which formed the roofs of these snug dwellings. Now they are mostly used as wine cellars, agricultural storage rooms or mushroom caves. The Romans made silos out of them at Amboise — *les greniers de César* or Caesar's granaries. The lowlands on each side of the river are rich in alluvium, which is why this part of Touraine is called 'the garden of

France'. Beyond these sediments are relatively poorer soils, the Gâtines whose name derives from the same source as the verb *gâter*, to spoil.

Past Tours and Angers the river makes for the sea. It skirts the southern margin of Brittany's ancient granite rock, bisects industrial Nantes, and passes the dockyards of St Nazaire before losing itself in the ocean at the wide estuary whose little resorts are lifted from obscurity by one, St Marc-sur-Mer. Here Jacques Tati made one of his memorable and moving comedy films, *Monsieur Hulot's Holiday*.

The Loire is France's longest river, some 1,100km of it. It is the fourth longest river in Europe. We are concerned with about a quarter of its length. Yet, unlike the Rhône, Seine, Rhine or Danube, it is commercially almost useless, happily for the traveller. Barges and other craft which once crowded the river have long since vanished. Few industrial complexes disfigure its banks, and there is no industrial pollution save where atomic power stations eject warm water into the stream. The tributaries, too, are uncontaminated. Time is slowed by the sense of peace and abundance these valleys emanate.

Countryside, Climate and Nature

In this great flood-plain there are almost no naturally dramatic features such as mountain folds, ravines or striking rocky outcrops. It is flat in the Sologne; elsewhere are gentle undulations whose high points nowhere reach 200m until you come to the rising ground east of the Aubigny-sur-Nère to Bourges road where some hills touch 300m. In a landscape of horizontal planes, the eye is drawn to the vertical lines of chalk cliffs set back from river banks.

Yet a view from the top of these modest escarpments provides a fresh perspective. At one's feet are the carpetlands of glinting rivers and an expanding horizon. From this gentle elevation you pick out each individual poplar tree along the river's edge. Beyond, the trees are compressed into dense foreshortened woodlands that hide the open parklands, meadows, heaths and farm-plots. A balanced, well-tempered panorama is laid out underneath a large sky. Nature looks to have been ordered by man, and that is near enough the case. The effect is to bring to mind a landscape painting of the seventeenth century, perhaps by the father of French painting, Nicolas Poussin. His portrait of the scene would have been deliberate and classical, with a literary flavour to it.

Without much difficulty the imagination can see a measured seventeeth-century picture from innumerable present-day vantage points. History, you can persuade yourself, began only 300 years ago, as the scene quietly erases millennia of turmoil and change. This is one of the subtle attractions of the Loire Valley. Intellectually, you know it has a long history, but antiquity does not walk constantly at your side as it does in Brittany or Provence, inescapably. It is easier to live in the here-and-now in the Valley. Even the châteaux do not overburden you with their past.

The châteaux are the architectural expression of this Renaissance landscape. Renaissance means rebirth, an emancipation from the trammels of medieval dogma to that modern outlook which goes by the name of humanism. The Renaissance had an important bearing on the Loire Valley, and still imbues its character, contours and peoples.

The people, here in the true centre of France, are like their landscape. They judge themselves reasonable, good-natured, well balanced. They live in a comfortable, indulgent land where sanity and moderation prevail. There is nothing over-stimulating. Anjou speaks of its *douceur angevine*. In Touraine, the 'Garden of France', they claim to speak the purest French; send your children here to learn the language.

How should the people of the whole region be called? Sometimes they are referred to as Vallerots. The people of Anjou are Angevins; those of Touraine, Tourangeaux; of Blois, Blésois; of Orléans, Orléanais. I like the name Ligerians for the inhabitants of the valley, for the Roman name for the Loire was Liger, and so the word has the ring of cultural homogeneity.

It is an area of moderate people, landscape and climate. One season merges into the next in gentle transition (as a rule). It compares with southern England's, save that the mid-summer months along the Loire tend to be warmer. For the visitor, it means a season which can stretch from April to November.

Spring comes early; the first wild flowers show at the end of February. A variety of early vegetables thrives in the temperate climate and fertile alluvial soil. A moist, warm wind prevails from the Atlantic, so that the average rainfall diminishes as you go inland. Frosts can recur into April, and short, sharp storms are not unknown in May and June. Summer is the period of high pressure systems over the Azores, but the Atlantic breezes moderate excessive temperatures. Typically, summer skies of Anjou and Touraine are wide, pale blue, dotted with cotton-wool balls of clouds, signs of fine weather. Delicate pastel colours of riverside buildings and trees reflect in the lazy waters of the rivers. Then, the Loire itself looks delectably placid. Slow, shallow waters slip past yellow, sandy islets sprouting

osiers. Clear yellow patches of sunlight filter through the light greens of poplars and willows. Note how the river banks have been built up with massive embankments (*levées*), constructed and repaired over the centuries to hold in the floods which used to devastate low-lying lands. In addition, they now keep open the riverside roads.

In winter, the serene river swells with the turbulent rush of water as rain and snow in the uplands drain into the Loire's huge catchment area which covers the whole of central France. Sand bars and islets are swept away; new ones emerge. Vast quantities of debris are carried down to make the Loire shallow and unnavigable.

As to natural history, it is broadly true to say that wild flowers, birds, animal and insect life are not so strikingly different from what southern England has to offer. Flora and fauna of the chalklands are similar to those of the English Downs.

Yet there are differences that quickly catch the eye. In the gardens, climbing roses, day lilies and morning glories consistently flower some weeks earlier than they do in Britain, a sign that here the temperatures are, on average, a shade warmer.

Along roadside verges you may suddenly come upon great carpets of light green and yellow euphorbias. Or else the scattered sentinels of tall asphodels stand on parade for hundreds of metres, their white flowers almost done and their stems turning to straw in early summer. To see commonplace plants and trees in a fresh setting gives them a fresh lustre; here is a thumb-nail impression of blossom time in late spring. Laburnum; lilac in its various hues; may; apple orchards; white and pink chestnuts; balsam; magnolias; regal irises as well as the yellow flag irises close to marsh and stream; brilliant fountains of chrome-yellow broom, here and there used as hedges; fields solid with buttercups; great clumps of cowslips; tamarisks; valerian; poppies; white and pink campions; ragged robins; dog daisies; vetches; clover; birdsfoot-trefoil; pink and blue violets; speedwell; scarlet pimpernels; the ubiquitous globes of mistletoe. Flamboyant dabs of purple-rose flowers add an exotic touch to the countryside; they are the Judas trees. I recall a high vertical cliff by the Loir. A startling column of Judas tree flowers rose majestically from the foot to the summit, one tree seeming to stand on the crown of another, the whole brilliant pillar set off by the dark foliage of other trees and shrubs clinging to the chalk banks.

Ecological pressures resulting from industrialisation and the intensification of farming have not been as great in the Valley as in England. A greater variety of indigenous species can flourish, and what is a rarity at home is sometimes more in evidence in our region. As an example, corn-cockles, corn-marigolds, cornflowers and orchids have been found in the vicinity of Troo on the Loir. There have always been more plant species here; their potential migration across the Channel became barred when the last land link with France disappeared into the Dover Straits 8,000 years ago.

In areas of intensive monoculture, diversity of wild life has been reduced. This is noticeable, for instance, where large fields have been given over to oil-seed rape crops. They are an attraction to some insect pests, and to hive-bees, but the rape imparts a somewhat disagreeable flavour to the honey.

River banks which have escaped too much human interference provide delightful glimpses and sounds of riverine bird-life from ducks to kingfishers. Hoopoes emit their hollow 'hoo-poo-poo' notes in the woodlands; the golden oriole alternates between a flute-like call and a raucous, cat-like cry. From the thickets come the liquid call and musical song of the nightingales.

The great diversity of bird life is in the lowland plateau of the Sologne. Its damp heaths and deciduous woodland contain many shallow, reed-fringed pools, the haunt of purple and night herons, bitterns, ducks, harriers, stilts, godwits, gulls, terns and warblers. Some of these birds can also be watched in the Forêt d'Orléans beyond the north bank of the Loire. In Sologne, take care not to trespass during your ornithological pursuits; you may be taken for a poacher.

In Sologne and wherever there are deciduous woods and small lakes are red and roe deer, wild boar, hares, pheasant and partridge. A nocturnal zoologist might come upon a genet. Beech martens, pine voles, edible dormice, red squirrels, have all been recorded in such habitats. Unknown in England are the bicoloured shrew and the white-toothed shrew.

Two unfamiliar species of bat, Kuhl's pipistrelle (which skims village walls and hedges with a fast, straight flight), and the Mediterranean horse-shoe bat are known to haunt the Valley.

Otters are seen not infrequently, especially on the islets along the quieter reaches of the river Vienne. In the muddy waters of ponds, ditches and gently flowing backwaters the European pond tortoise is sometimes seen. Again, in moist places at night you will hear the pure piping notes of the midwife toad.

For the entomologist, the spring air is filled with the penetrating song of crickets in uncultivated fields. Equally loud but rougher are the bursts of stridulation from great green bush-crickets of an afternoon or night in late summer. Good fortune may let you find

Fishing in the Cher where birdlife is plentiful

a praying mantis (likely to be the green variety; brown specimens are seen more frequently in the south), adopting its myth-laden spectral pose. Here, the species is at the northern limit of its range.

At a rough estimate, three dozen species of butterfly occur in the region which are not indigenous to Britain. Fritillaries, graylings, blues, skippers can be seen during their flight periods of first or second broods. The lepidopterist may even come across the scarce swallowtail (*le flambé* to the French), flying in early or late summer, perhaps among the orchards, or laying its eggs on fruit trees or sloes which are the larva's food.

Among moths, the death's head hawk moth is more likely to be met with than in Britain. Many species of the beautifully shaped and marked hawk moths or *Sphingidae* are not uncommon; the humming-bird hawk moth (*le moro-sphinx*), darting from flower to flower in the daytime, never fails to enchant. The great peacock moth (*le grand paon de nuit*), the largest European moth and

normally thought of as a southern insect, occurs occasionally at night in vineyards, orchards and parklands.

There is a great diversity of habitats for the different families of beetles. Ground beetles in rotting trees and moist fields; water beetles in the pools; rove beetles under stones or in mushrooms and decaying vegetation; glow-worms in moist grass; stag beetles in oak woods; chafers in flowers; dung beetles in animal excrement; long-horned beetles in woodlands or meadow flowers. These are only some of the showier beetles. Some are becoming scarcer as their natural habitats are lost. Over-collecting has helped the decline of many insect species. Specimen-hunting for the cabinet has become as anti-social an activity as is collecting rare birds' eggs.

Approaches to the Loire
Some point along the Loire Valley can be reached within a day's car drive from any of the French Channel ports: Dunkerque, Calais, Boulogne, Dieppe, Le Havre, Cherbourg, St Malo and

SOME LEISURELY ITINERARIES FROM THE CHANNEL PORTS

(Numbers on the left are the relevant Michelin maps)

51 **Calais** — Guines — Hardinghen — Le Wast — Desvres — Hucqueliers — Hesdin —
52 Frévent — Doullens — Albert — Roye —
56 Lassigny — Compiègne — Crépy-en-Valois — Meaux — Couilly —
61 Fontenay — Trésigny — Melun — Fontainebleau — Nemours — Château-Landon — Montargis —
65 **Gien** 439km

52 **Dieppe** — Arques-la-Bataille — Torcy-le-Petit — St Saëns —
53 St Denis-le-Thiboult — Fleury-sur-Andelle — Les Andelys — Vernon — Pacy-sur-Eure — Anet — Dreux — Chartres —
60 Patay — **Orléans** 274km

55 **Le Havre** — Pont de Tancarville (toll bridge) — Pont Audemer — Lieurey — Bernay — Broglie — La Trinité-de-Réville — Mélicourt — La Ferté-Frêne —
60 L'Aigle — Les Aspres —

Mortagne-au-Perche — Bellême — Le Ferté-Bernard — Vibraye —
64 St Calais — Montoire-sur-le-Loir — Château-Renault — Neuillé-le-Lierre — Vouvray — **Tours** 310km

54 **Cherbourg** — Bricquebec — St Sauveur-le-Vicomte — La Haye-du-Puits — Coutances —
59 Villedieu-les-Poëles — St Hilaire-du-Harcouët — Landivy — Ernée —
63 Laval — Château-Gontier — Ménil — Daon — Marigné — Querré — Feneu — **Angers** 275km

59 **St Malo** — Châteauneuf-d'Ille-et-Vilaine — La Vicomté — Dinan — Béchéel — Rennes —
63 Châteaubriant — Candé — **Angers** 209km

58 **Roscoff** — St Pol-de-Léon — Penzé — St Thégonnec — St Saveur — Huelgoat — Carhaix-Plouguer — Rostrenen — Pontivy — Josselin —
63 La Chapelle — Malestroit — St Gravé — Redon — Lancé — Plessé — Nozay — Riaillé — St Mars-la-Jaille — Ancenis — **Angers** 387km

Roscoff. Consequently, the choice of routes is very nearly limitless, from toll autoroutes to winding lanes.

If you want to get somewhere quickly, take the autoroutes (speed limits 130km/h when the road surface is dry, 110km/h when wet). Outside Dunkerque the A25 goes on to join the A1 to Paris. The A26 is the autoroute for both Calais and Boulogne; it also links with the A1 which leads into the *Boulevard Périphérique* round Paris to bring you on to the A10 (*L'Aquitaine*) which serves Orléans and the Loire

Valley towns between Orléans and Tours, before crossing the river in the direction of Poitiers and Bordeaux. From the port of Dieppe you can pick up the A13 south of Rouen which allows you to meet with the A10 in Paris. Similarly, from Le Havre, after you have crossed the handsome Tancarville toll bridge, you join the A13. Motorists aiming for places further west in the Valley, such as Saumur or Angers, can turn off the A10 southwest of Paris and continue on the A11 as far as Le Mans or even Laval, and then take the N23 (from Le Mans) or N162 (from Laval) southwards. Calais to Orléans is 414km, and Calais to Tours 529km.

If you prefer not to take your own car, self-drive arrangements can be made through one of the international car hire companies in Britain, or else with a car hire agency in France. Main tourist offices will be able to supply names and addresses of the latter. Fly-drive is easily arranged from any airport in Britain on flights to Paris, or else in conjunction with the seasonal Air France Heathrow to Nantes service. Travellers by train can obtain from French Railways (SNCF) an inclusive rail plus car-hire ticket, the car being collected at the destination (larger railway stations only).

Travellers entirely without a car will join one of the many Loire-bound trains from Paris. Most fast services are from the Gare d'Austerlitz to Orléans, Blois and Tours, or Orléans, Salbris, Vierzon, Bourges. The main-line station for Orléans is Les Aubrais-Orléans, and for Tours, St Pierre-des-Corps; frequent trains to the respective city centres take about five minutes.

Another route to Tours is from Gare d'Austerlitz by Vendôme, 248km in $3\frac{1}{2}$ hours. For Angers, go to Paris (Montparnasse); the route is via Le Mans (308km in $2\frac{1}{2}$ hours). The fastest trains on all these routes have first and second class seats, and are named — *Etendard, Montaigne, Aquitaine, Aunis, Le Drapeau*, for instance — and a supplement is charged. The *Jules Verne*, a crack TEE (Trans Europ Express), non-stop between Paris and Angers, is first class only.

Stopping trains on the main lines give access to many smaller towns and villages, particularly those along the north bank of the Loire between Orléans and Angers. Of the branch lines, Tours is the centre from which the largest number of rail excursions can be made:

The ideal region for a cycling holiday

Tours — Loches; Tours — Azay-le-Rideau — Chinon; Tours — Chenonceaux — St Aignan — Vierzon — Bourges; Tours — Château-du-Loir. Other local lines are Saumur — Montreuil-Bellay, and Salbris — Romorantin — Valençay.

Travellers aiming for the eastern end of the Loire Valley must go to Paris (Gare de Lyon) for the 155km run to Gien via Montargis.

SNCF and associated private companies run bus services from railway stations or nearby bus stations (*gares routières*) to small towns and villages in the area. Orléans, Tours, Bourges, Saumur, Blois and Salbris are rail/bus

14

termini from which these services, with the train networks, effectively cover the whole of the Loire Valley.

Train travellers should buy holiday tickets (*'France Vacances'*); they are valid for seven or fifteen days or a month, giving unlimited first or second class rail travel throughout France. Tickets bought in France must be validated (*composter*) at the orange-coloured automatic date-stamping machines at platform entrances. If you omit to do this, you may be liable to a 20 per cent surcharge.

Few regions lend themselves better to a cycling holiday. Miles of riverside roads, country lanes and gentle gradients make for unstrenuous enjoyment. You can take your own bicycle by train, or else you can arrange for a hired bicycle to await you at one of a number of railway stations; this can be booked when you buy your railway ticket through French Railways. Alternatively, when you are at your holiday centre you can walk into a bicycle shop — many towns and villages have them — and hire a machine for as many days as you require it.

During the summer season, a number of tour operators in Britain offer inclusive tours by coach. Most take in Paris and a few of the major châteaux, and the tours are usually for five or eight days. Regular coach services between London and Tours are run by Euroways.

Half and whole day coach excursions from the bigger tourist centres are run by various operators including SNCF, and details about the latter's programmes can be had at both railway stations and *gares routières*. Setting out from Paris are *'Châteaux de la Loire'* coach tours by SNCF, American Express, Cartour, Cityrama and Wagons-Lits Cook.

Inclusive packages for self-catering stay-put holidays with accommodation ranging from privately owned châteaux, farmhouses, to cottages or flats, are available. Some of them can be booked through *Gîtes de France* at the French National Tourist Office in London or New York. On-site caravans or tents are also packaged by a certain companies in Britain and America.

In this unhurried countryside the leisurely visitor reaps the best rewards. Look at the Michelin map. Innumerable lanes meander in a network and do not seem to hold a promise of anything particularly interesting. In reality, when you come to them, they lead off invitingly from the more populous riverside main roads and drift into stretches of market-gardens, orchards, nurseries, farmlands, meadows and water meadows, parklands, woodlands, ponds, scrub and open country. Some of these lanes are signposted *'Route Touristique'*. Follow them. They lead to quiet and charming spots. Wine-lovers should look out for roads marked *'Route du Vin'* for a circuit of well-known vineyard names. Long stretches of the Loire have a road running along each bank. If the grass on the opposite bank looks greener, there are thirty-two road bridges between Angers and Gien; you are not confined to one side of the river for long.

In this book, the Loire and its tributaries are followed upstream, beginning with the environs of Angers and ending at Gien. Some might prefer to reverse the itinerary, but the upstream method is my own preference. The reason is that if you take a route east of Paris and aim to strike the Loire at Gien you come first to the uglier side of the town, and the view of the Loire is both unexpected and relatively uninteresting, and you deprive yourself of the quite beautiful and dramatic view, and the sense of elegant harmony which the

At Gennes; one of the many road bridges across the Loire between Angers and Gien

graceful arches of the bridge provide from the western side. More importantly, coming down to Gien in this way robs you of a proper preparation and anticipation of the Loire Valley.

Descend through Normandy on the western side of Paris and the introduction unfolds slowly. You do not come at first to the Loire but to the Loir. As the pronunciation of the two is the same, confusion is avoided by referring to them as La Loire and Le Loir. For many travellers Le Loir is the lovelier river because of its more intimate atmosphere. For myself, Le Loir is the 'dormouse river', for that is the other meaning of *le loir*.

The routes from Normandy make you aware of leaving the cooler, more acid, cider-making soils. The south beckons. In the widening landscapes the light, surely, becomes clearer, the sky higher. On the chalklands, the slopes feel drier

as rainwater drains quickly into the valley bottoms. You see the first modest vine-rows, harbingers of the fine wines of Anjou and Touraine to come. You are approaching that river in the middle of France where north and south meet.

The word 'château' recurs, inevitably, in this book. A note as to what it defines may not be out of place. No single word in English adequately translates 'château'. We employ numerous words that differentiate the various kinds of châteaux. We speak of feudal fortress, castle, stately home, palace, country house, manor house, country mansion. In French, 'château' is a convenient blanket-word for all such buildings both large and small. More specific identification in French involves the introduction of such terms as *château-fort, gentilhommière* or *manoir*, for whom the generic word 'chateau' is mostly used in the first instance.

In this 'château-country' you will

want to see at least one or two examples. Unless you are an architectural specialist, use restraint. A holiday can be spoiled through the mistaken belief that all the famous châteaux have to be 'done'. Such excess induces boredom and the glazed look which archaeologists playfully diagnose as *mal-de-mur*. A holiday can be enjoyed to the full with no more than some casual contemplation of châteaux from outside the gates. Apart from anything else, entrance fees for a family can mount up. Moreover, it must be said that some châteaux are not very stimulating; nor are the guides; nor are the furnishings. If you are there during the summer season, choose at least one château which puts on a *son-et-lumière* display, for this can really be an experience.

Drives through the countryside will inevitably bring you upon tucked-away buildings, some of them privately owned and not always open to the public. Such places can be admired from a distance or from the entrance gates, to add further pleasure to general sightseeing.

More earnest students of history will find that the Valley invites the devising of itineraries which follow a specific theme. The most obvious is a route which takes in the places associated with the Plantagenets who occupied the English throne from 1154 to 1485. Some places have links with Scotland. Follow in the footsteps of Joan of Arc through the Orléanais and Touraine. Or trace the medieval pilgrimage routes that went through Vendôme, Troo and Tours to meet up with those coming from Orléans and Blois before going on south to St James of Compostella. You can plan a tour round the prehistoric monuments; the Roman remains; the vineyard roads; the windmills; those with a literary bent can visit the places associated with Rabelais and Balzac.

To gain an overall impression and understanding of the whole region, the motorist who has, say, ten (preferably more) days at his disposal, can think of staying at three different centres. He might begin with three nights in Anjou, either in Angers or somewhere in the surrounding country. Then three nights in the centre of the region, in Touraine, in or near Tours. For his last three nights, he could establish a base further east, in or near Gien or in the heart of the Sologne. In this way, his diet need certainly not consist of *châteaux* alone.

HOTELS, FOOD AND WINE

Hotels, from Grand to Simple

As elsewhere in France, hotels in our region are classified by the French Government Tourist Authority according to the amenities provided. At the upper end of the scale are the luxury ('palace') and world-famous establishments, officially graded as ****L. Top class hotels receive **** for comfort. Very comfortable hotels are classified with ***. A good average hotel is **, while a simple yet still comfortable hotel is *. By and large, the cost-scale descends with the smaller number of stars. These ratings are not of themselves assessments of quality.

The Loire Valley's long-standing popularity is reflected in the diversity and density of hotel accommodation. Many annual guides are published to help you decide. There are bland, official lists which take care not to show preference. There are publications by hotel chains which, naturally, extol the virtues of their members. Incidentally, the phrase 'hotel chain' can be misleading, for it implies a standardised architecture or administration. There are modern, functional hotel chains in France, such as Campanile, which work to a definite and admirable formula. The majority of 'chains', however, are loose associations of highly individualistic owners and managers, whose hotels are endlessly diverse in every respect; they simply organise themselves into a chain for the benefit of their own trade and customers.

To begin at the top: it is still possible to find luxury, comfort, service in stylish surroundings. They cost a great deal and can be an experience worth the outlay. *Relais et Châteaux* fill the bill. Their annual, illustrated guide proffers a glimpse of grandeur. Nine of them are represented in our region:

Auberge des Templiers at Les Bézards (Loiret);
Le Prieuré at Chênehutte-les-Tuffeaux (Maine-et-Loire);
Château de Marçay near Chinon (Indre-et-Loire);
Château de Teildras at Cheffes (Maine-et-Loire);
Domaine de Beauvoir at Luynes (Indre-et-Loire);
Château d'Artigny at Montbazon (Indre-et-Loire);
Domaine des Hauts-de-Loire at Onzain (Loir-et-Cher);
Hôtel d'Espagne at Valençay (Indre);
Grand Hôtel Lion d'Or at Romorantin-Lanthenay (Loir-et-Cher).

Perhaps not quite so prestigious, yet aiming for a discriminating clientele, are the hotels which belong to *Châteaux Hôtels Indépendants*; it, too, issues an illustrated handbook every year.

Most readers, I assume, will be looking for more modestly priced and perhaps homelier places to stay at. The region is liberally endowed with hotels that answer this description. Seasoned travellers to France use the annually revised red *Guide Michelin France*. It has maintained its reputation since early this century for solid reliability and compactness of information, its

limitations set by an innate bourgeois conservatism notwithstanding. Apart from anything else, its indispensability for the touring motorist who has not booked his accommodation lies in stating which days of the week a hotel closes — a rather important consideration these days.

Travellers who must keep a watchful eye on what they spend will appreciate the annual guide of the *Logis et Auberges de France* (published in March and free to callers at the French National Tourist Office; for it to be sent a postal charge is made). This highly condensed and unadorned book contains more than 4,500 small hotels and inns, mostly in country towns and villages. The simplest inns are the *Auberges* where a room can cost as little as £5 a night, and a meal less than £4, or dinner, bed and breakfast £10. They may not always come up to *Michelin* criteria, but they are bargains for the budget-conscious.

A word of caution: as I have explained, French hotels are awarded stars for their comfort. If you visualise a one- or two-star hotel, for instance, to be comfortable in the sense of being equipped with cosy, relaxing public rooms, rather as we expect them to be at home, you may be disappointed. Lounges, bars, television rooms tend to be uncomfortable and stark by English standards. Traditionally, we have placed emphasis on comfort before food in our hotels; the French have taken the opposite viewpoint; our respective conventions are beginning to converge.

When you telephone or write to book a room, you may be asked to send a deposit (*verser des arrhes*). This understandable precaution on the part of the hotelier arises out of the lamentable fact that an increasing percentage of travellers do not turn up to honour their booking. If you reserve a room for the same evening, the hotelier may ask you to arrive not later than six o'clock, after which time the room will be let to the first caller. Especially during the high season it is advisable to allow for unexpected delays in driving to the hotel.

Half-board arrangements with the hotel satisfy most people. You are free to spend the whole day sightseeing. If you stay three nights or more, favourable half-pension terms may well be available. Some hotels, especially in larger towns, provide only bed and breakfast; this is convenient if you want to try out different restaurants each day. My own preference is to eat in the hotel's restaurant unless its cuisine is not up to standard, so as to get to know the character and atmosphere of the place better, and to judge the variety of its menus.

Hotels apart, self-catering in flats, farms, rural houses (*gîtes ruraux*), holiday villages, youth hostels, international holiday centres for young people, arts and crafts courses, activitiy holidays, camping and caravaning: all provide a remarkable diversity of accommodation and experience.

The Loire at Table

If ever one man, through his satirical inspiration, stamped a gastronomic image on a region, it was François Rabelais when, in the sixteenth century, he wrote his *Gargantua*. Gargantua, and Rabelais' own name, have passed into everyday language as universal symbols of grossness and exuberance of the appetites, but his native Touraine's reputation for hearty eating has remained ever since. Gargantua was born, it may be remembered, out of his mother's left ear after eleven months of gestation (a prescient fantasy of genetic engineering), during a riverside feast near Chinon. Villagers had been invited from all around to celebrate the event

Holidays in harness

with a meal of tripes of fattened beeves. Then they danced, and then they took a 'light' repast of more mountains of food and flagons of wine.

In the old days, on Rabelais's home ground, to get 'as fat as a monk' seems to have been commonplace enough, and gluttony was compounded by a tooth which craved sweets and cakes as well.

Nowadays, I dare say Rabelaisian and Gargantuan *bons viveurs* are no more common in Touraine than anywhere else. In any event, the distinction of the regional cuisine lies in its simplicity. It is a curious fact that no outstandingly great regional dishes have sprung from

Part of the old kitchens at Château de Montgeoffroy

the Loire Valley. Yet, historically, it was the birthplace of French cuisine. Just as the Loire Valley absorbed, then modified the sixteenth-century Italian Renaissance architecture introduced by Catherine de Medici as queen-regent of France, so it at first copied, then subtly altered the work of Catherine's Italian chefs. While the monarchs of France either ruled from their royal châteaux along the Loire, or else returned to them for relaxation from Versailles, gastronomic standards were maintained. Sophisticated Paris is so near by way of autoroutes, and food conscious visitors descend annually on the valley. They help to sustain those standards, as the ratings in *Michelin* and other gastronomic guides confirm.

A benevolent climate and soil ensure the abundance of vegetables, fruits and vines; forests provide the game; rivers and meres the fish. The ingredients for a restaurant meal of quality are always to hand. The least expensive *menu touristique* is likely to offer simple, standard dishes (though cheapness is not necessarily a bar to quality ingredients and careful cooking). If food interests you, be prepared to pay more, and look out for regional specialities.

Shad (*alose*), either stuffed (*farcie*) or with sorrel sauce (*à l'oseille*); pike (*brochet*) served with a creamy butter sauce with wine vinegar and shallots (*beurre blanc*). Pike is a ubiquitous fish, and may appear as delicate *quenelles de brochet* (a light, sausage-shaped soufflé) or as young pike served like whitebait. Loire salmon (*saumon*) is considered to be among the finest in France, though there may be less of it now; *saumon à la Chambord*, cooked in red wine, is a sought-after delicacy. Eels (*anguilles*) appear frequently on menus. They may be stewed in wine on their own or with other fish to make a *matellote*, or else fried whole in breadcrumbs with other small river fish to make *friture de la Loire*, or yet again minced and baked and served cold as *terrine d'anguille*.

Pork, the chief local meat, is served traditionally with prunes (*noisettes de porc aux pruneaux*). Sologne, south of Orléans, is the main source of game: hare *(lièvre),* Sologne jugged hare *(civet de lièvre de Sologne*), rabbit (*lapin,* or young rabbit, *lapereau*), boar (*sanglier*) in autumn and winter. Many varieties of pâté are produced.

Of the many vegetables grown locally, asparagus (*asperges*), broad beans (*fèves*) and cardoons (*cardons*), rather like a large celery are especially good.

Specialities associated with towns are numerous, but they are not always easy to come by. *Andouillettes*, chitterling sausages from Angers and Jargeau, as well as *andouilles* (cold smoked sausages); *boudin de volaille à la Richelieu*, a sausage made of truffles, mushrooms and chicken; *cernaux au verjus* is a Touraine *hcrs d'oeuvres* of green walnuts in grape juice, sait, pepper and chervil; *chouée*, a dish of cabbage and butter is an Angevin delicacy; *jambon de volaille*, chicken legs stuffed with ham from Richelieu; *quiche Tourangelle*, open tart of minced potted pork, the latter being the delicately flavoured *rillettes de Tours; rillauds*, cooked pieces of breast of pork, served hot at Angers; *beuchelle à la Tourangelle*, mushrooms and cream with kidneys and sweetbreads; *truffiat*, potato cake. Orléans' contribution is its mustard and wine vinegar.

Apples, pears (William pears are used in an *eau-de-vie*), peaches, plums of Tours, strawberries of Orléans, melons of Langeais, quinces, cherries (especially from Olivet), dessert grapes, and an apricot-peach known as *alberge de Tours*, are some of the Ligerian fruits. Various sweet dishes are made with them. Apples stuffed with jam and baked are *bourdaines*. In Anjou, cherries are called *guignes*, and a *guignolet*

liqueur is made from them. Angers is the home of Cointreau where many fruit liqueurs are produced. A pear in syrup with liqueur and ice-cream is *poire belle angevine*. Slices of caramelised apples or pears covered in pastry make *tarte des Demoiselles Tatin*. A not uncommon jelly is made of quinces and is called *cotignac* (those of Orléans are said to be outstanding), and a quince cheese is also made (*pâté de cotignac*), to say nothing of an *eau-de-vie des coings*.

Cheese boards and specialist shops display an interesting variety of cheeses. Goats' cheeses are commoner than cows'. Of the former, there are *Ste Maure*, soft, cylindrical, with a pronounced goat flavour, and is sometimes called *chèvre long*; similar to *Ste Maure* are *Villebarou* and *Ligueil*, all at their best between May and November. *Romorantin* (or *Selles-sur-Cher*) is dark, blue-skinned and nutty. Similar cheeses come from Troo and Montoire. *Valençay* (or pyramide because of its shape) is firm, medium strong, nutty; so is *Levroux*. *Crémets* are small fresh goat cheeses, eaten with sugar and cream, a speciality of Anjou; they can also be mixed with cow's milk. *Gien* is a dumpy cylindrical mixture of goat and cow. There is a goat's cheese biscuit, *sablée biquette*.

The chief cow's milk cheese is *Olivet-bleu*, factory-made and innoculated with mould. It is small and circular, sometimes wrapped in leaves, and best between October and June. *Olivet-cendré* looks similar, and is ripened in charcoal ash, its best eating period being between November and July. Closely related are *Vendôme bleu* or *cendré* (October to June), *frinault affiné, Villiers, St Benoît* (the latter's surface is rubbed with salt and charcoal).

Since Renaissance times, the occupants of the châteaux, wealthy, leisured, cultivated, developed a fondness for sweet things. The tradition of making such delicacies or *friandises* continues, whatever the warnings about dental caries and heart disorders. Today's sweet buns or *fouaces* were favoured by Rabelais; there are the *macarons* of Cormery and almond cakes of Vouvray. Gâtinais honey has long been well known. Château-Gontier prizes its *croquettes anisées*; Montoire and Romorantin their *croquets*; Blois its chocolates; Beaugency its liquorice *réglisses*; Angers its *biscuits anisées*; and from Bourges come *forestines* and *amandines*.

As a result of the close connection between the kings of England and their lands in Anjou and Touraine, Loire wines have for long been familiar to the English nobility and merchants. They liked their Loire wines white, sweet and strong. They were known as Andegavie wines which had been transported first to Nantes and then carried by sea to English ports.

At home, Loire wines are growing in popularity. They are light, crisp, pleasant, untaxing to pass judgement on, and are mostly relatively inexpensive. Some experts say that the Loire *vins de table* are superior in quality to their counterparts from elsewhere in France. On holiday, local wines taste ambrosial; take them home and they may disappoint. Is it that they do not travel, or is our taste-bud memory deceived by the travelling? However it is, Loire wines delight by their diversity and youthfulness. None have the gravity of Burgundy or Bordeaux wines. Few can be rated as 'great'. A great wine has a venerable history and tradition compressed within the bottle. Loire wines are like the landscapes that make them: the sense of the past is only wine-skin deep and their personality is youth

Grape harvest in Touraine

and spontaneity, even though some Loire wines like Sancerre begin to take on a Burgundian character, and Coteaux du Layon, a Bordelais.

Sancerre — delicate, refreshing and very nearly a great wine — is, strictly speaking, outside our area. So, too, is Muscadet — that deliciously tart accompaniment to fish — which comes from nearer the mouth of the Loire. Muscadet and Sancerre appear on every wine list, so both must be mentioned.

But before a wine survey, a few points may be worth making. Expensive wines are not necessarily the most enjoyable complement to a meal. Local ones can be appropriate even though they do not have an *Appellation Contrôlée* (AC) which guarantees the authenticity of the bottle's contents. Some of the cheaper

wines, both *Vin Délimité de Qualité Superieure* (VDQS) — regarded as inferior to AC wines — and the modest *Vin de Pays* which specifies the *département* or area it comes from, are often very good indeed.

As I have already hinted, we must cheat a little to include Muscadet. It is a recognised accompaniment to fish and shellfish, and fish is always prominent on menus, so Muscadet will be drunk frequently. Muscadet is also an aperitif; when added to *cassis* liqueur it makes that satisfying summer pre-dinner drink the French call *Kir* which is more potent than the taste suggests. The vineyards lie on the south bank of the river, to the east and went of Nantes. Muscadet Sèvre-et-Maine is best known. It should be drunk young, like a *Beaujolais de l'an*,

23

and when it tingles faintly on the tongue it is quite an inspiring wine. *Gros Plant du Pays Nantais* (VDQS) tends to be treated as a poor relation to Muscadet. It is light and dry, a little more acid than Muscadet, and also goes well with fish in general and oysters in particular. Its extensive vineyards are southwest of Nantes, beyond those of Muscadet.

The first wine-producing area properly within our region is the Coteaux d'Ancenis, making a light, dry rosé. From around Angers come other rosés, the dry *rosé du Loire*, the slightly sweet *rosé d'Anjou*, and the sweet *Cabernet d'Anjou*. When Loire rosé wines are dry they can be almost raspingly so. Still on the north bank of the river are dry white wines with a rich 'nose', the Savennières (Coulée-de-Serrant and Roche-aux-Moines) which, because of the smallness of the vineyards, command very high prices. South of Angers, the Coteaux du Layon are sweet white wines which go well with quail or ham.

Saumur is the next district; its vineyards spread south beyond Montreuil-Bellay. Some red wine, fruity in good years, is produced, though Anjou generally is not much associated with red wines. Saumur whites are the abundant crops, maturing in the natural chalk caves which are cool enough to demand warm clothing even on a hot summer's day. Saumur sparkling bears more than a passing resemblance to champagne, for the grapes are grown on similar soil; it is very decidedly cheaper than champagne. *Anjou pétillant*, a faintly sparkling rosé is also made.

Entering Touraine, and surrounding the towns of Chinon and Bourgueil, are vineyards which produce two famous wines. North of the river the dark red fruity Bourgueil carries, the French aver, a scent of raspberries, but it is hard to pin a precise name on it. Chinon wine, from both sides of the river Vienne, was Rabelais' native tipple, and that is said to smell of violets. Bourgueil and Chinon are not easy to tell apart. Both are supple and fragrant; perhaps Bourgueil is a little more robust, and Chinon softer. You are supposed to drink Chinon out of a special glass, a round bowl curving outwards towards the top. Such glasses can be bought in Chinon shops with Rabelais' head and shoulders etched on the glass, along with a quotation from the great man: *Beuvez tousjours, Ne mourrais jamais* (Keep drinking, You'll never die). Try drinking both Bourgueil and Chinon chilled with *hors d'oeuvre*, and *chambré* with a main course of white meat.

Moving north of Tours to the river Loir, you come to the Coteaux du Loir, mostly dry white wines. Clos de Jasnières, with a tiny and sought-after output, is fruitier and slightly sweeter than most wines of the Loir valley, and resembles Vouvray. In the vicinity of La Chartre-sur-le-Loir are the wines of La Chartre, Marçon, Ruillé and, for a little innocent oneupmanship, you can refer nonchalantly to Vouvray, not *the* Vouvray on the Loire, but Vouvray-sur-Loir, a village three kilometres east of Château-du-Loir. Further east again are the Coteaux du Vendômois wines. With the exception of Jasnières, a quality wine, they are fun to try and compare though they may not be easy to come by.

Return to the larger vineyards of the Loire. The Sauvignon de Touraine is dry, flowery and inexpensive; the best of the genus is the aromatic Azay-le-Rideau. Touraine Gamay is a red wine made from the same grape as Beaujolais, and their flavours are not unlike. The wine museum in Tours deals with the social history of the regional wine-vine.

East of Tours is Vouvray whose *route du vin* starts at Noizay, eight kilometres further east. Vouvray's sparkling *vin mousseux* is, along with those of Anjou, Touraine and Montlouis, an *Appellation Contrôlée*. One dry (*brut*) Touraine is called *vin vif* instead of *mousseux*. Grapes in the Vouvray area are harvested late — towards the end of October — for the bunches to become infected with the 'noble rot' fungus, *la pourriture noble*, which makes the skin shrivel and the grape dry out to produce the sweet yet sharp still wine, whose quality varies from year to year. On the opposite side of the river to Vouvray, the Montlouis vineyards produce a sparkling wine which is saddled with the doubtful label of 'poor man's Vouvray'.

At Amboise, some red and a dry rosé are made. Thereafter come the less distinguished *vins de l'Orléannais* and Coteaux du Gennois. Yet in the seventeenth century the English esteemed the wines of Orléans. They were red and yellowish wines which were spoken of as 'clarets' and reckoned to be among the best in France. They were strong and recommended to be drunk by those gentlemen who suffered exhaustion after 'too much use of women'.

Away from the Loire itself are small and interesting vineyards which have to be searched out, for they are true local wines which are sold only in the district, for the most part. Quincy and Reuilly, west of Bourges; Valençay and Cheverny (the latter appears on some hotel wine-lists); Menetou-Salon (rather like Sancerre), are examples. Just beyond our boundaries are the famous vineyards of Sancerre and Pouilly-sur-Loire where the delectable Pouilly-fumé comes from.

To sum up: a stimulating array of wines, varied in character and flavour, deriving from the small variations and blends of soil — clay, chalk, alluvium, sand, pebbles — of the river valleys, where the *vins du pays*, drunk perhaps as a carafe wine, can be of surprising agreeableness.

Alcohol in relation to health and illness is one of the obsessions of our times. As a tailpiece, therefore, I will mention a few wines which can help in the treatment of specific disorders, according to some homeopathic authorities. Light, moderately acid white Anjou wines stimulate a jaded appetite. A quality sweet Anjou wine or Vouvray are indicated for sufferers from dyspepsia, flatulence and constipation because of the small quantity of sulphur dioxide preservative in these wines. Muscadet is beneficial in arteriosclerosis, the homeopaths say, because the vines are grown on decalcified soil. Saumur wines, stemming from a calcareous soil, help rectify calcium deficiency, while a light Saumur white is used for its diuretic and slightly alkaline properties in the treatment of chronic nephritis. Sancerre and Pouilly wines seem to be beneficial for many conditions. As they grow on silica, they are used for dealing with gallstones, gout and high blood-pressure. Sancerre, they say, should be drunk if you put on weight, a condition a prolonged stay in the Loire Valley might encourage.

HISTORY IN BRIEF

Traces of Pre-history

Primitive stone implements have been unearthed in many places. They testify to the presence of small human communities along the banks of the Loire and its tributaries between 400,000 and 150,000 years ago during the Lower Palaeolithic. Museum drawers supply the evidence of flint tools, the small differences of whose working are of significance to specialist pre-historians. Yet lay curiosity is aroused. How did these unknown people eke out a living?

How did they adapt during cycles of great climatic changes when the vegetation and the creatures it supported also altered radically? Adaptation seems to have been skilful. Stone tools were modified to allow effective hunting of new species of game which the changed environment nurtured.

Periodically, other small groups of people migrated into the region and brought with them original ideas, so that alien and indigenous cultures fused. For the most part, as long as the environment remained the same there was little incentive to improve on existing tools and techniques. Nor could our region emulate the magnificent cave art of Périgord further south, for the soft chalk provided neither the durable surface nor the constancy of temperature and humidity which the limestone caves and *abris* (rock-shelters) supplied to their Upper Palaeolithic contemporaries.

The last Ice Age moved away northwards some 10,000 years ago.

Dense forests covered much of the region. Men hunted, gathered berries and fished in the wider, shallower and more placid waters of the rivers. Deer antlers were fashioned into harpoons. As the climate grew warmer, the big mammals left, and new tools, suited to trapping smaller mammals such as rabbits, had to be invented.

The Loire has always been the highway by which cultural innovations and destructions have been introduced, moving downstream in the direction of the Atlantic. In the fourth millennium an invasion which had its origins in the Danube basin introduced stock-raising: cattle, pigs, goats, sheep and dogs. It was a product of the so-called 'Neolithic Revolution' which had begun in the eastern Mediterranean and, probably independently though later, in Provence. Europe's economic and social structures were transformed by the revolution. The Loire peoples resisted it for a while for the good reason that theirs was chiefly a forest industry unsuited to a pastoral

Prehistoric megalith at Bagneux, near Saumur, one of the largest in France

system. But a cooler, drier climate — the Sub-boreal — superseded the previous moist, warm Atlantic phase, and forest clearings were more easily created. Stock-raising established itself, though on a relatively small scale. Wheat and barley were introduced in the Early Neolithic, but agriculture was confined to the plateaux where wind-born loess — fine, fertile dust — reduced the density of the woodlands and prepared the way for the rich granary-lands of the Beauce today.

The Danubian settlers built large rectangular wooden houses, erected the first funerary monuments — passage graves or *dolmens à couloir* — and identified their differing cultures through distinctive types of pottery.

Round about 2,500BC — the Middle Neolithic — megaliths of the Loire developed a characteristic Angevin form by which a simple portico replaced the traditional passage, and the monument became more elongated. Some very large megaliths can still be seen. The one at Bagneux ouside Saumur is one of the largest in France. Those outside Gennes are not much smaller. By taking the D571 east from Angers in the direction of Saumur, you will be able to seek out a number of dolmens and menhirs. Or, north of Tours, is the massively impressive dolmen outside Mettray, hidden by a copse, called *Grotte aux Fées*. The same question always springs to mind: how did Neolithic man transport and erect these gigantic slabs of rock?

Less spectacular Neolithic remains can be searched out. They are the *polissoirs*, boulders on which stone axes were regularly sharpened. Usually found near streams, these hard buff-stones betray their one-time function by the smooth parallel grooves, striations which have survived for 5,000 years. You are most likely to come across them

in the very north of the region where it abuts the Beauce.

Were they the work of a branch of the Mediterranean Ligurian tribes to which the classical authors of antiquity referred? Liguria is a name still given to the Italian Riviera. Liger was the name of the river Loire to the ancients. It is surely not mere coincidence that Ligurian and Liger sound alike. In all likelihood, the Ligerians or Ligurians were the peoples of the Loire. They seemed to understand the influence of sun and moon on the fertility of the soil. They planted their crops by the waxing and waning of the moon. Loire Valley farmers followed the same principle into this century.

In the Late Neolithic — the period between 2,500 and 1,700BC — at Le Grand Pressigny (a little south of our area) was a 'factory' which exploited easily worked and high quality flint. It turned out large daggers, new types of arrowhead which were leaf- and lozenge-shaped and tanged, exporting these articles all over Europe. The *Musée de la Préhistoire* in the château at Le Grand Pressigny is an important one and gives a very good idea of the Stone Age implements produced in the vicinity.

As long as tools were made of stone alone, there were great limitations imposed on development. True, local communities did extend their farming activities to less fertile soils, and the exploitation of the land began to take on a pattern which was to persist for many centuries. Their dwellings must have been built of very light materials, for no traces of them have been found. Nor did they leave any grave-goods.

Gold and copper ornaments and copper daggers appeared, as well as high quality beaker-ware. The source of diffusion of this culture is still a matter of conjecture. The people who brought the Beaker Culture seemed to infiltrate

Bronze boar from pagan temple at Neuvy-en-Sullias, in Musée Historique, Orléans

into populations of the late Neolithic and had no territories of their own. The Chalcolithic (copper) culture was superseded by bronze. The Bronze Age lasted some 1,200 years until about 600BC. It was an important development for the Loire Valley where metal-working centres were set up. Bronze is an alloy of copper with a high percentage of tin, and the latter was mined extensively in the lower reaches of the Loire. A vigorous export trade in flanged axes and palstaves flourished. During that time collective megalithic graves gave way to individual cremation in urns which were placed in cemeteries by the Urnfield peoples who spread westwards along the Loire and its tributaries between 1,100 and 800BC. Fertility figures which had been widely worshipped by Neolithic peoples lost out to more abstract symbolism which, it has been suggested, was a cult brought about by metallurgy with which was associated the sun and fire.

Long-distance trade routes were established, for copper and bronze came originally from the eastern Mediterranean. Bronze Age Phoenicians sailed up the Loire to trade in them. Hoards of copper ingots have been found near Bourges and Azay-le-Rideau. Metalwork was taught in the Valley, and craftsmen spread far and wide from there. Metalware was also imported from England and Ireland. Axes, swords and bronze ornaments were constantly evolving until the arrival of the Iron Age, between 800 and 600BC, made many of these artefacts obsolete. The Iron Age produced superb craftsmen. Trade expanded still further. A general rise in the population of France was probably shared by the Loire region, coinciding with a rise in the average annual rainfall which increased the productivity of the crops.

With the approach of the written record of history a general picture emerges of a thriving Ligerian civilisation, its industries and outlooks modified by both peaceful and violent invasions from the innovative east. Among the most influential of these invaders were the central European Celts. Between 1,200 and 800BC, the Celts, called *Carnutes*, founded Chartres, Orléans, Blois, Amboise, using the rivers Loire and Cher for commercial traffic. Mining, metallurgy and farming prospered. A lively society, evidently, but politically backward, as was to be demonstrated in their confrontations with the Romans.

Caesar and the Roman Conquest

As the Roman conquest of Gaul moved northwards, Caesar's soldiers found themselves facing muscular, tall, blond Celts who belonged to an aristocracy which enjoyed luxury and military heroics. Their shields and weapons were magnificently decorated; their warlike rituals were Homeric and blood-curdling. These were the men who hurled contemptuous insults across the lines at the small, dark Romans. They were headstrong, valorous, hardworking, quarrelsome and inconsistent. They revered their Druids and their poets. Each chieftan was surrounded by a faithful band of personal followers. Peasants, herdsmen and artisans who did not belong to the élite and were probably not muscular, tall and blond lived in scattered villages and farms.

The Ligerian region belonged to that large area of Gaul, between the Rhine, the Cevennes and the Atlantic coast, which was known as *Gallia Comata* ('Long-haired Gaul').

Caesar resolved to conquer the whole of Gaul in 58BC, and the tribes of the Loire submitted without much resistance. They did so in part because their neighbours, the Aedui who held central Gaul up to the east bank of the Loire where the *département* of Nièvre now is, had been allies of Rome since 123BC, and were recognised as 'Friends and Allies of the Roman people'. The other Gaulish tribes were the Namnetes on the north side of the Loire estuary and inland beyond Nantes; the Pictones occupied the other side of the river. The Turones (around Tours) straddled the middle Loire and the Cher, making of Tours their main river-port built on pile foundations. North of them were the Andecavi.

The Carnutes held the land between what is now Paris and Orléans

(*Genabum*), building the riverside port here, as well as at Amboise and Blois. The Celtic name for Blois was *Bleiz* or *Blaiz*, which was 'wolf' in Celtic, an indication of the inhospitable, wolf-infested forestlands of the Blésois. To the south, the Biturges had *Avaricum* (Bourges) as their capital.

By 52BC unrest had spread among the tribes. They swooped on *Genabum*, 'led by two desperadoes', writes Caesar in his *Conquest of Gaul*, killing the Roman traders who resided in the town. The news of this event, which took place at dawn, was known in Auvergne, 150 miles away, before eight o'clock of the same day, Caesar comments. By shouted words across field and hill, from one village to the next, was the intelligence carried.

Caesar came from Italy to quell the uprising. *Genabum*, which guarded a bridge across the river, was quickly captured and the booty distributed among the Roman troops. Then Caesar marched into Sologne to make the difficult attack on *Avaricum* (Bourges), perhaps camping, as some historians think, at Romorantin, as part of his struggle against his main enemy, Vercingetorix.

In the course of his campaigns in the Loire Valley, Caesar had boats built at Nazelles (*Navicellis*), a village behind Amboise, in preparation for his attack on Tours (*Turonum*). During the final rebellion in 52-51BC, Caesar again had to fight in the vicinity of the Loire during a particularly cold winter which he turned to advantage by billetting his soldiers in the relative comfort of his headquarters at *Genabum*, while the Celts suffered the elements out in the open. Further skirmishes, further victories for Caesar. Having satisfied himself that Gaul was pacified, he laid down generous conditions of subjection. 'By these means it was easy to induce a people exhausted by so many defeats to live in peace', he concludes in *The Conquest of Gaul.*

Roman occupation brought many material benefits. Agriculture was improved; the vine was introduced. Roads were built. The main highway was that from *Lutetia* (Paris), the capital of the Parisii tribe, through *Genabum* (Orléans), along the north bank of the *Liger* to *Caesarodunum* (Tours). From here, one road led south to *Limonum* (Limoges) and Aquitaine. Another continued along the north side of the Loire to its mouth. Some of today's arrow-straight roads follow the Roman foundations.

Tax-gathering was left to local magistrates. Under Emperor Augustus, the Loire became the boundary between the northern province of *Lugdunensis* and the southern one of *Aquitania*, to remain the political division for 300 years. Prosperous towns were concentrated on the river which was heavily used for the transport of goods. Major towns, like Orléans, commanded bridges over the river. New towns, as a rule, were given a name which incorporated both a Latin name and a Celtic suffix such as *magus* (market) or *dunum* (stronghold). Tours, which had been *Altionos* to the Gauls, became *Caesarodunum Turonum* to preserve the tribal name. Angers, previously *Andegavi*, capital of the Andes tribe, became *Juliomagus Andecavarum*. Many other towns today betray a Celtic origin in their names. In all, the region was lightly populated, and during the 300 years of Roman domination, it prospered and stayed at peace.

In place of the one-time Gaulish kings, already being discarded before the Roman conquest, there were elected magistrates or *vergobrets*, but powerful chiefs still ruled over their broad lands and commanded private armies.

As was customary under Roman rule, local religion was respected as long as it did not contravene Roman law. Roman deities were imported. Gaulish Druids — wise men drawn from the ruling classes who maintained Celtic traditions and myths and held powers of life and death — had to be removed; they were seen as a potential source of political unrest. The Druid's annual meeting point had been at Fleury, a suburb of St Benoît-sur-Loire, their consecrated ground at the 'umbilical centre' of Gaul.

Of the handsome Roman towns and their public buildings which were essential to Roman garrisons — baths, aqueducts, arenas, amphitheatres — not much remains by comparison with Provence. Yet there are more fragments than might be imagined.

A few examples will serve. In the basilica of St Benoît, the chancel floor is a Roman mosaic brought from Italy. In Orléans, the base of the Tour Blanche is Gallo-Roman. A section of the city wall and a round tower of Tours, built about AD275, have been exposed. A little to the west of Thésée (*Thascica*) on the Cher, is a Roman ruin called 'Mansio de Manselles'. It had been a *mansio*, or staging-post of Roman troops on the road between Bourges and Tours. *Thascica* was marked on the famous Peutinger map of the third century, and such *mansiones* were sited roughly every forty kilometres. A Roman *cippus*, a cylindrical pagan altar, with carved warriors round it, is in the church of St Ours in Loches, doing duty as a font. North-east of Luynes are thirty-five columns and several arches of the Roman aqueduct which supplied Tours with water. Eight kilometres west, at Cinq Mars-la-Pile, stands a massive square tower on the top of a cliff; its function is still a matter of speculation. At St Maur, the abbey, founded in the sixth century, stands on the site of a

Basilica of St Benôt-sur-Loire, site of Druids' 'umbilical centre' of Gaul

Roman fountain whose basin is beneath the chapel; lead pipes and some of the bases of the Roman arches are visible. At nearby Gennes, fragments of an aqueduct and *nymphaeum*, and the foundations of an amphitheatre have been revealed, all suggesting that Gennes had been an important station in Roman times. There were baths and an arena on the Evière hill at Angers, almost entirely destroyed during the rebuilding zeal in the last century. Archaeologists have excavated the sites of Gallo-Roman houses in the Sologne. One at Millançay in the Forêt de Bruadan (a name of Celtic origin), and another at Montrieux-en-Sologne, suggest that the basis of Solognot agriculture was cattle in open pastures, rye and vines in the clearings.

The Coming of Christianity

Some authorities think that an evangelist, Altin, came to this part of central Gaul to convert the inhabitants to Christianity as early as the first century. He is said to have arrived with Savinius, one of the seventy-two disciples sent by the apostle Peter. Similarly, St Maurice came to Angers. St Gatien went to Tours a little later as the first, but clandestine, bishop of Tours. When Constantine the Great was emperor in the fourth century his conversion to Christianity made it the official religion of the Roman Empire.

St Martin was the most famous of all evangelists in the Loire Valley. He, like all the other evangelists of those times, had been a soldier with the Roman legions. All were 'foreigners'; St Martin was Hungarian. This arose because the Romans recruited men from Greece and Hungary to protect the frontiers of Gaul from invasion by Germanic tribes. St Martin was still wearing Roman uniform when he cut his cape in half to give one part of it to a beggar. Living a frugal life in the chalk caves of Marmoutier, he was elected bishop of Tours and founded the

31

Hermit caves below Abbey of Marmoutier, used by St Martin, fourth-century evangelist of Loire Valley

abbey of Marmoutier in 372. So great was his popularity with the people of Tours that on his death the city became a major focus of pilgrimage. A whole town, 'Martinopolis' had to be built a little to the west of Gallo-Roman Tours to accommodate the influx. A visit to the cave cells of St Martin, St Gatien, St Denis, St Brice and St Patrick is part of the tour of Marmoutier Abbey.

Once the Roman defences of Gaul had given way, the Loire Valley, after centuries of stability, fell prey to invasions. Asian and German hordes came from the east. First, Attila the Hun, then Childeric and the Franks. The Franks, of Teutonic origin, erstwhile vassals of Rome, crossed the Rhine and, under their young king Clovis (he came to the throne at the age of fifteen in 481) captured much of northwest France. Orléans became his capital. Later, this daring and ruthless man became a Christian, partly to please his determined wife, partly to obtain the support of the Church. During his conquest, he halted his armies on the north bank of the Loire at Amboise. On the opposite bank lay the territory of the Visigoths under Alaric who had acquired the once Roman province of Aquitaine. In 503 the two kings met, choosing as neutral ground the Ile d'Or (now a camp site) in the middle of the river. They swore eternal friendship. Milestones on mounds of earth, known as *donges*, marked the boundary, and one such mound is still visible at Sublaines, south of Amboise. Four years later, Clovis fell on the Visigoths at Vouillé, killed Alaric with his own hands, and drove the enemy almost to the Pyrenees.

Clovis died in 511. His kingdom of the Franks was not unlike the territory of France today. He had thrown back the Huns from the gates of Orléans in 451 under the inspired leadership of the bishop of St Aignan. Clovis had run his kingdom like a private estate, so that on his death that estate was parcelled out among his sons. This dynasty of Merovingian kings became weaker both politically and genetically and the dynasty ended in 752, but not before the Arab advance from Spain had been crushed. In 751 they had reached the plateau north of Poitiers. Their defeat by Charles Martel ('the Hammer') finally destroyed Musulman aspirations in northern France.

Under Charlemagne (742-814) literature and learning flourished. Priories and churches were built. At the abbey of Cormery, founded in 791, lived and taught Alcuin of York who came to love the Loire Valley. Alcuin, perhaps

Chinon

Horse-riding in Loiret

Château of Villandry

St Aignan-sur-Cher

the most distinguished scholar of his day, taught the emperor's family and members of the court. He came to Cormery in 796, continuing to spread his civilising influence until his death there in 804. A similar influence was wielded by Bishop Théodulfe who founded the first university at Orléans and gave free lessons.

Charlemagne reigned for forty-six years, and the Loire region was but a tiny fragment of his great empire; Normandy and Brittany were not part of it. Fragments of the Carolingian presence are the mosaic in the church of Germigny-des-Prés; another was found beneath Orléans cathedral. A ninth-century church is in the crypt of St Solenne in Blois. There are others in Tours, St Benoît-sur-Loire, Bourgueil, Cravant and Chinon.

Abbeys and priories were a cultural counterflow to the chaos which constant wars and local warlord quarrels threatened. Not only were they centres of religious observance, they also served as places of refuge. They were seats of learning where ancient texts were preserved, studied and copied. They were shelters and hospitals for travellers and pilgrims. In their gardens they often tried out new methods of agriculture. Marmoutier was one of the most prestigious abbeys in Christendom; Cormery's prominence can be attributed to Alcuin. The Benedictine abbey of St Benoît-sur-Loire had been founded in 650 and was at its peak under Charlemagne and Charles the Bald in the ninth century. Orléans, too, was an important centre. Finally, there was the Chartreuse du Liget, founded by Henry II of England in reparation for the assassination of Thomas à Becket at Canterbury.

When the Frankish empire of Charlemagne collapsed, east Franks became Germans; west Franks became French. The frontier between them was never clearly defined, so there are those who have argued that this oversight sowed the seeds of 1,000 years of

Germiny-des-Prés church contains treasures brought by Charlemagne

Loches keep, built in eleventh century by fortress builder Foulques Nerra

hostility between France and Germany.

Feudal Anjou and the Crown of England
Charlemagne's successors lacked his charismatic power to hold together his racially disparate empire. Through the laws of inheritance the empire was divided into three kingdoms. What we know as France, excluding Brittany, became the Kingdom of Charles. The king was too weak to defend his peoples and repel the Viking-Norman invaders who landed at the mouth of the Loire and ravaged all the lands between Nantes and Orléans. The first king of the Capetian dynasty, Hugues Capet (938-96) hardly dared move out of his capital of Orléans. Real power lay with his feudal vassals such as the Counts of Anjou, Touraine, Blois and Maine. They did as they chose: raised armies, built castles, appointed bishops and minted their own money. War between one county and another was incessant. Fortresses were everywhere erected as a consequence of these disputes.

Supreme among the fortress builders was Count Foulques III, known to all as Foulques Nerra, The Black Falcon (971-1040), a skilful general who built innumerable square keeps at high speed, mainly to serve his feuding with his neighbour, the Count of Blois. First, he put up temporary constructions of wood, a stockade on top of an earthwork, known as a *plessis*. This name recurs in these parts, although all signs of the original forts have disappeared. Permanent stone fortresses replaced the *plessis* at strategic points. Those at Loches, Montbazon and Montrichard are among the remnants of Foulques Nerra's handiwork.

In those early, cheerless, cramped stone keeps, everyone ate and slept on the first floor. By the thirteenth century fortresses were becoming more spacious with separate kitchens and bedrooms, a change introduced by Crusaders returning from Palestine. As more refined instruments of war were devised, square towers gave way to round ones to reduce the efficacy of grappling-hooks. Walls were reinforced to thwart the sappers. Angers' massive castle sums up medieval ideas on defence. Not until the sixteenth century did gracious palaces begin to supplant the castles, where moats and dungeons were more decorative than useful. A century later, châteaux were designed for social ostentation and amusement, surrounded by ornamental gardens.

The name of Foulques Nerra begins the tangled history of Anjou and the kings of England. Anjou had come into existence in the seventh or eighth century; Foulques I was the founder of a bellicose Angevin family. A later Foulques fought Henry I of England, and his son Geoffrey married Henry's daughter Matilda in 1129. Out of this union came Henry Plantagenet (the name derives from the habit of the first counts of Anjou of wearing a sprig of *genista* — broom — in their hats), born at Le Mans in 1133.

By the age of eighteen, Henry had inherited Normandy, Anjou and Touraine (ceded to France in 1242). When Louis VII of France divorced his young and vivacious wife Eleanor in 1152, Henry Plantagenet thought that marriage to her would aid his interests. Before it happened, a touch of romantic farce crept in. Henry's younger brother, only sixteen, took a fancy to Eleanor, twelve years his senior, and tried to kidnap her. Then the son of the Count of Champagne attempted the same at Tours. Eleanor evaded them both, married Henry, her former husband's arch rival, and brought Aquitaine as her dowry. Henry ruled from the English Channel to the Pyrenees. On the death of King Stephen in 1154 (himself a count of Blois), Henry acquired the throne of England as grandson of Henry I and great-grandson of William the Conqueror. By such quirks of circumstance did he become Henry II of England and eight Plantagenet kings ruled until the death of Richard II in 1399.

He spent half his life in France. Eleanor, her relations with Henry cooling, set up her own court in Poitiers. She urged her sons John Lackland and Richard Coeur-de-Lion to side with the French king against their father. Henry II died at Chinon in 1189 during the struggles with his sons. He, Queen Eleanor and Richard I all have their tombs at Fontevraud Abbey. When John Lackland succeeded his brother Richard as king of England, he lost Anjou to King Philippe-Auguste of France, for it to be recaptured under Henry V and Henry VI. In 1444, Anjou returned nominally to France, though the king's direct rule of the duchy did not take place until 1584.

Joan's route through the Loire Valley can be traced only very approximately, but to follow her zigzag course by car or bicycle is a congenial way to get to know the hidden aspects of the Ligerian countryside. From Gien, which she reached on 1 March, 1429 after crossing hostile Burgundy territory from Vaucouleurs, to Chinon, which she reached on 6 March is about 240km.

Gien — St Gondon — Viglain — Sennely.

Sennely — Vouzon (where there is a *Chemin de la Pucelle*, Path of the Maid) — Lamotte-Beuvron — Ste Marie — St Viâtre — Faverolles — Château de la Noue — La Ferté-Imbault — Selles-St Denis — Les Anges — La Brillière — Mennetou-sur-Cher.

Mennetou-sur-Cher — St Loup — St Julien-sur-Cher — Selles-sur-Cher — St Aignan — Orbigny — Genillé — L'Ile Auger — Chanceaux-près-Loches.

Chanceaux-près-Loches — Dolus-le-Sec — Montfoué (somewhere in the fields hereabouts is said to be a *Chemin de Jeanne d'Arc*, along which corn does not grow, according to legend) — Manthelan — Mazère —

Le Carroir-Jodel — Ste Catherine-de-Fierbois.

Ste Catherine-de-Fierbois — St Epain — Crouzilles — St Gilles — Chinon.

At Chinon, Joan recognised the Dauphin in spite of his disguise. At the end of March she was taken to Poitiers for a three-week examination of her 'humility, virginity and honesty'.

21 April, left Chinon along today's *Carrefour de la Pucelle*, to Blois for blessing of her standard by Bishop of Reims.

29 April, entered Orléans.

30 April, inspected Orléans on horseback.

6 May, attacked English in Bastille des Augustins, wounded in foot.

7 May, wounded in shoulder; Orléans relieved.

8 May, triumphal entry into city.

After returning to Tours and Loches, Joan liberated Jargeau on 12 June, and Beaugency on 16 June.

18 June, defeated English under Sir John Talbot at Patay.

22 June, Joan and Dauphin pray at St Benoît-sur-Loire; they stay at Château de Sully where she pursuaded him to go to Reims for his coronation.

For quite a long time, then, the kings of England wielded as much, if not more, power in France than did the French kings. The court in England was as French as was the French in France.

Last of the Angevin dukes was 'Good King René' under whose rule the duchy flowered. His court at Angers was brilliant and Angers, for a short while, found itself a major European town. His kingship was the titular one of Sicily; his other fiefdom was Provence, and he died at Aix-en-Provence in 1480. His wide learning, his gentle manner and genuine concern for his people's welfare made him much loved but unsuited to political intrigue and military decisiveness which his responsiblities demanded. He avoided the castles of Angers and Saumur, preferring to stay in the small manor houses which he had built or bought at Chanzé, Rivette, Ponts-de-Cé, Belligan, near Angers; Launay outside Saumur; La Ménitré on the Loire; Beaufort and Baugé close to the forests where he could hunt.

One of the last counts of Blois was so debt-ridden that he sold his country to the Count of Orléans, and in 1498 Blois was incorporated into the kingdom of France.

Orléans, from the tenth to the sixteenth centuries was either the capital of the French 'royal demesne' when it was virtually confined to the Ile de France, or else second capital to Paris until the last of the Orléans-Angoulême dynasty in Henri III.

Technically, the English monarch in his French territories was a vassal of the king of France. In practice, he was often the more powerful. Constant territorial disputes between them and repeated English invasions of France, helped foment the Hundred Years' War (1338-1453). Attacks and counter-attacks were punctuated by truces and realignment of allies. It was a brutal and desolating war. In 1422 the English entered Paris; Orléans was invested; the English, with their Burgundian allies, possessed all northern France except Brittany.

French morale was low, leadership from their king, the Dauphin as Charles VII was called until his coronation, lacking, for he was a pathetic, haunted creature. Weak and vacillating, ill-fed, dressed in wretched clothes, without money, he scuttled from one château in the Loire to another. In 1429, Joan of Arc appeared. She lived only nineteen years (1412-1431). Driven by her 'voices' she confronted the Dauphin at Chinon. She was allowed to join the forces mustering for the relief of Orléans. Without any position of command, she

placed herself at the head of the army in full armour. Orléans was relieved. This defeat of the English was the turning point in the war. The English were pushed out of the Loire Valley with the recapture of Beaugency and Jargeau, and defeated at Patay. The impetuous Joan then led the Dauphin through hostile country for him to be crowned at Reims. During an ill-advised attack on Paris, Joan was wounded. Then the king's money ran out and he disbanded his army for the winter. In 1430, she was captured by the Burgundians at Compiègne, sold to the English who had her tried for sorcery by the Inquisition, and found guilty. She died at the stake in Rouen. Charles VII raised not a finger in her defence. The Maid was canonised in 1920. Her impetus continued to give the French heart for further attacks on the English. The latter lost Normandy and Bordeaux; the Burgundians became less enthusiastic allies; all that was left to the crown of England was Calais. The Hundred Year's War dragged to its dishonourable conclusion.

Wealth and Renaissance

After Joan of Arc had been put to death, Charles VII, no longer merely 'King of Bourges' as he had been sarcastically called, but King of France, developed into a powerful monarch. He created a strong, well paid army which put down his nobles' private wars; he effectively reorganised the tax system. For this, he enlisted the help of an immensely wealthy merchant of Bourges, Jacques Coeur (1395-1456). Almost single-handed he restored the prosperity of France. In Bourges, his monument is his superb *hôtel*, in whose attic roof can still be seen the pigeon loft; pigeons were his means of keeping in touch with his agents all over Europe.

Jacques Coeur, as Controller of the Mint, court banker and controller of the

Bourges, mansion of merchant Jacques Coeur, who revived France's prosperity in fifteenth century

king's finances, wielded vast power until in 1451 he was falsely charged with complicity in poisoning the king's lovely mistress, Agnès Sorel, who had been installed in the château of Loches. Coeur left France to die on the island of Chios. He was not a nobleman. He represented a new class of successful merchants — the bourgeoisie. The bourgeoisie was to stamp its character on the Loire Valley.

King Louis XI (1423-83) resided in the grim fortress of Plessis-lès-Tours. Like his father, Charles VII, he surrounded himself with prosperous businessmen who bought themselves vast acres in Touraine. Louis' Controller of the Treasury was Jean Bourré who built himself the Château of Plessis-Bourré which combined medieval defences on the lower floors with comfort, light, air and space provided by large windows above. For the château had to receive the king and his court from time to time

and provide entertainment. Tours, Blois, Langeais, Chenonceau, Azay-le-Rideau, Villandry, Le Clos-Lucé are examples of châteaux built by the powerful financiers of the day. They also bought town mansions and renovated them to standards of appropriate magnificence.

Rulers held court in their various royal châteaux: Angers, Blois, Plessis-lès-Tours, Amboise, Loches, Chambord, Chinon. To be near the king, the merchants dotted their châteaux along the Loire, the centre of political, financial and religious decisions. Here were concentrated the shrewdest and most ambitious figures who salvaged the nation's economy and stimulated diverse industrial enterprises. Louis XI himself introduced mulberry trees, silkworms and silk-making to the region.

Towards the end of the fifteenth century the Italian Renaissance found its way into the Valley. Charles VIII (1470-

98) had invaded Lombardy (his troops included Scottish archers). When he was forced to retreat he brought back with him Italian artists and art treasures as loot. Everything Italian became fashionable, though the architectural assimilation was slow, yet harmonious, as can be seen at Chambord, Azay-le-Rideau and mansions, such as Hôtel Pincé in Angers and Hôtel d'Alluye in Blois. High Renaissance was the apogee of flaunted luxury. The stimulus to ostentation was the intense rivalry between courtiers.

The Italians introduced major innovations in architecture, sculpture, medal-making, embroidery, gardening, gastronomy. Two of the most famous Italian artists were Francesco Laurana and Girolamo della Robbia. The latter's well-known terra cotta medallions which he produced at Orléans were much in demand. Yet all the Italian art, transplanted from the strong light of Italy, fell under the influence of the gentle light of the middle of France, to become modified into an indigenous style (much as it was in England).

Leonardo da Vinci (1452-1519), the universal genius, was brought to Amboise by François I (1494-1547). He worked at Le Clos Lucé for the last three years of his life. Among his imaginative projects were plans for a canal between Tours and Lyon. He had schemes to improve the Loire region. Many of his plans can be seen at the museum of Le Close Lucé. Amboise's reputation was immensely heightened by Leonardo's presence there.

The most significant political influence was Catherine de Medici (1519-89). By her marriage to Henri II she exerted much authority as queen, while after his death in 1559, she was a queen-regent with absolute power. She was almost the embodiment of the Italian Renaissance in France. Her well-intentioned policy of equal support for Catholics and Protestants contained the seeds of its own destruction. Caught in a web of intrigue of her particularly

Langeais, built by powerful financier in fifteenth century

odious family, she was disliked by most ordinary French people, and sneered at as a tradesman's daughter by French nobility.

Great native talent arose at the same time. The lyric poet Pierre de Ronsard (1524-85), born near Vendôme, and François Rabelais (1495-1553), physician and satirist, a native of Chinon, added further lustre.

Below the appearance of opulence lay latent conflict. Catherine de Medici had been unable to resolve the growing intolerance and bitterness between the rapidly enlarging faction of Protestant Huguenot dissidents and Catholics

supporting a weak monarch. The Wars of Religion broke out in 1562. Murder and abductions were commonplace. Blois, Orléans and Amboise (where Catherine de Medici and Mary Stuart witnessed the slaughter of Protestant plotters) were the scenes of massacres and reprisals. Churches and abbeys were sacked by the Huguenots. Henri IV's Edict of Tolerance, prepared at Angers and signed in Nantes in 1598 brought peace, but the Edict was revoked eighty-seven years later.

With the death of Catherine de Medici the vitality began to ebb from the Loire Valley. The royal châteaux were used

Statue of Louis XII, 'the bourgeois king of Blois', at Blois, a fine example of Renaissance architecture

the district. The manufacture of steel at Amboise was established by the Duc de Choiseul.

From Revolution to the Present Day

Theoretically, the Loire Valley ought to have been the scene of particularly intense bitterness as France erupted towards the Revolution of 1789. Despotic government, corruption, maladministration, unfair tax burdens, favouritism towards the clergy, class privilege and greed brought about unrest. In the Valley, absentee landlords visited their châteaux for pleasure and ostentation, neglecting their estates and the workers on them. The aristocracy was chiefly concerned with hunting. As that majestically shrewd observer, Arthur Young — Britain's first agricultural minister — noted at Amboise in 1787, 'Great lords love too much an environ of forests, boars, and

less and less. The court moved to Versailles. Temporarily, existing industries suffered a decline only to revive and expand, for the river remained the cheapest form of transport. Sugar refineries appeared between Nantes and Orléans. Loire and Seine rivers were linked by the construction of the Briare canal. Distilleries were set up. Canvas factories were established at Angers. Saumur made cotton goods. Printed fabrics were in such demand that Nantes, Angers and Orléans were all turning them out. In addition, Orléans had factories making stockings and vinegar. Later, in 1790, the first steam-driven cotton-spinning machinery was installed in all three towns. The Duc de Penthièvre, grandson of Louis XIV, instituted a silk factory at Châteauneuf-sur-Loire as part of his benevolent scheme to provide work in

Catherine de Medici's chamber in Blois château

huntsmen, instead of marking their residence by the accompanyment of neat and well cultivated farms, clean cottages, and happy peasants.'

There were a few notable exceptions among the noble landowners; some sympathised with the aspirations of the revolution. Little good it did them; their heads rolled with the recalcitrants.

Yet the violence in the Valley was less than might have been expected. It is a recurring feature of Ligerian history that most insurrectionist movements since Roman times tended to arise on the instigation of outsiders. The margins rather than the heart of the region experienced the main upheavals. Perhaps this reflects a tolerant nature and an inner poise among the Ligerians. As far as the 1789 revolution is concerned, it can also be said that there was less poverty than elsewhere. Vineyards flourished; the soil encouraged intensive cultivation, even though there were huge expanses — the Sologne in particular — which were dismally uproductive.

In the wake of the Revolution itself many factories closed and industries declined. Some vindictive and haphazard desecration of châteaux by Republican extremists — the sans-culottes — took place. The properties of Catholic Royalists were sequestered. Angers embraced the heady notions of revolution with enthusiasm. Its cathedral was sacked and renamed a 'Temple of Reason'. People in the towns tended to favour the revolutionaries; the peasants the monarchy. Numerically in the minority, the rural population communicated clandestinely by means of signals telegraphed by the sails of windmills of which Anjou has as many as any region in France. Many can still be seen in the vicinity of Angers and southeast and southwest of Saumur.

Outraged at the execution of Louis XVI in 1793, at the persecution of the clergy, and at mass *levées* for the Republican army, an insurrection flared at St Florent-sur-Loire. It spread to Angers and south into Vendée, and the Vendée War was conducted by Catholic Royalists (the 'Whites') against the Convention (the 'Blues'). Following the defeat of the Royalists in 1794, the Republicans shot or guillotined thousands in Angers. Not until 1801 was reconciliation achieved, through the indefatigable work of the Angevin, Abbé Bernier who was made Bishop of Orléans by Napoleon. The Valley settled down to a compromise administration within its new *départements*; Republicans dominated the towns, Catholics and Royalists the country where they rebuilt the châteaux, retained the *métairie* system whereby peasants farmed the land and shared the profit with the landlord, bred cattle, and ensured the livings of the rural priests.

In spite of the lesser revolutions of 1830 and 1848, general prosperity continued through the development of rural industries. Napoleon III ordered drainage and replanting in the once fever-ridden Sologne. The same man, unhappily, blundered into war with Prussia in 1870. The French were defeated at Sedan; the Emperor surrendered; Paris was invested. Tours was made a capital from which the national defence was conducted by Gambetta who had escaped from Paris by balloon. The Germans advanced as far as the Loire where a French force awaited them at Orléans and was driven back. Briefly, on the road to Blois, the tiny 'Army of the Loire' replused the Germans only to be defeated soon afterwards. Tours was bombarded and then occupied.

In World War I the Loire played its traditional role as an outpost of Paris, to fall back on in times of reverse. Tours

The Loire at Saumur, now a peaceful, uncommercial river

was a base for United States troops.

War again; in 1940 the treasures of the Louvre were stored in the château of Chambord. Tours became the temporary seat of the French government. Here the question of an armistice was seriously raised for the first time. Orléans and Tours were heavily damaged by bombardment, by the Germans in 1940, later by Allied air forces. In a few weeks of 1940, French military resistance was crushed and for a

time all was chaos. At Saumur, the tiny, ill-equipped force of the Military School, ignoring orders to retreat, held three Loire bridges for more than twenty-four hours before running out of ammunition and able-bodied cadets. On 24 October 1940, Montoire on the Loir was chosen as the meeting-place between Adolf Hitler and the aged Marshal Pétain, Head of State of what was to be known as the Vichy Government. They met in a railway carriage in the station, near a railway tunnel, in case the RAF should attack the town. The river Loire became the boundary between occupied France to the north and unoccupied France to the south.

There is, by the way, a devious connection between the Cross of Lorraine, the emblem of the Free French Forces under General de Gaulle, and Anjou. At Baugé is the Chapelle des Incurables which possesses a large, double-armed, ornamented wooden cross brought back from Constantinople by a Crusader, and said to be a relic of the true Cross. This cross became the heraldic emblem of the Counts of Anjou. From them, it passed to the House of Lorraine to become the Cross of Lorraine.

Post-war, Tours and Orléans have been extensively reconstructed, and both towns have expanded enormously. Traditional rural activities continue to flourish: vines, fruits, vegetables, mushrooms, flowers, and all the delicacies of the table, and the new crop of oil-seed rape advertises its brilliant yellow flowers from afar. Well-established industries stand side-by-side with newer ones: printing, pharmaceuticals, glass-works, perfumeries, metallurgy, shoe-making, nuclear energy plants. Orléans university is large and American in style. The government aims at decentralisation — a bone of contention of many years' standing. Orléans, so easily reached from Paris, represents the first logical place for such a policy to be applied,

and, as a result, the Valley has kept in step with the general post-war prosperity of France.

What is paradoxical, however, is that today's prosperity is achieved without the river Loire being able to fulfil its age-old part as a trading highway. Now it is unused save for occasional pleasure boats. Gone are the powerful guilds which ensured the rights of their members to make a living transporting goods along the river. Gone are the tolls and levies and the various designs of boats able to navigate the idiosyncracies of current and shoal. Chief vessel in the past was the *chaland*, flat-bottomed, without a keel, steered by a massive oar and pole. The Musée de la Marine de la Loire at Châteauneuf-sur-Loire reconstructs the history of river life.

Railways, of course, destroyed the commercial value of the river. They came in 1846. Steamboats plied between Orléans and Nantes, but their boilers blew up. Even when the splendidly named *Inexplosibles* were launched trade had already dwindled below the level of profitability. The last effort to use a steam tug to ferry cocoa and sugar to the Blois chocolate factory of Poulain was abandoned in 1908. As embankments were strengthened to stop flooding, the river's current became faster and more capricious. Well-surfaced roads along the embankments finished the Loire as a commercial highway. It comes down to us now as the decorative artery of the region.

1 Angers and Round about_

With a population of 141,000 Angers is the largest town in the region (although the conurbation of Tours makes that city considerably larger). Most of the interesting places are compressed within the old town of Angers which is bounded by broad, tree-lined boulevards. The bigger section of old Angers is behind the east bank of the river Maine where the castle and cathedral are. Two bridges continue the boulevards across the river.

If you wish to make Angers the headquarters for leisurely sightseeing on foot there are numerous hotels within or just outside these boulevards. Distances are not great. Motorists who prefer to stay in the countryside yet within easy reach of Angers will find agreeable hotels at Cheffes, Matheflon, Les Rosiers, Gennes, Chavagnes, Brissac-Quincé, Rochefort-sur-Loire, Le Lion d'Angers, all in a radius of 30km from Angers. In the city itself metered parking places are quite close to the chief sights.

As you drive into Angers, the castle is the dominating landmark and the first place to make for. Its presence is

Some of the seventeen bastion towers of Château d'Angers

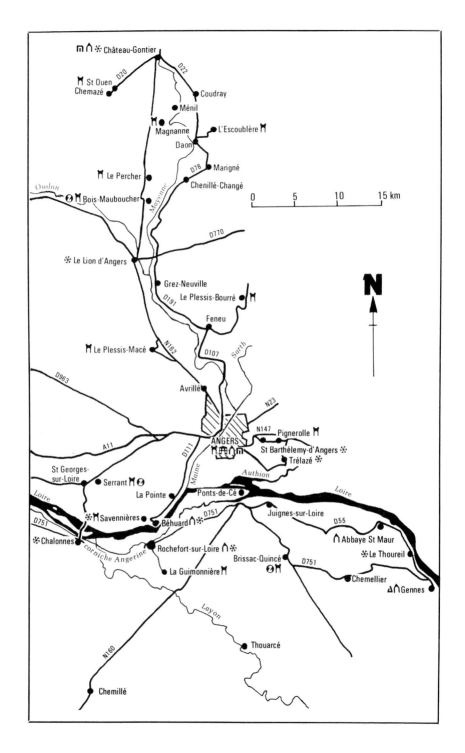

Château-Gontier

St Ouen
Chemazé

D20

D22

Coudray

Ménil

Magnanne

L'Escoublère

Daon

Le Percher

D78

Marigné

Chenillé-Changé

Oudon

Bois-Mauboucher

0   5   10   15 km

Le Lion d'Angers

D770

Grez-Neuville

Le Plessis-Bourré

D191

Feneu

N

Le Plessis-Macé

N162

D107

Sarthe

Mayenne

D963

Avrillé

N23

ANGERS

N147

Pignerolle

St Barthélemy-d'Angers

Trélazé

St Georges-
sur-Loire

A11

D111

Maine

Serrant

La Pointe

Ponts-de-Cé

Authion

Loire

Juignes-sur-Loire

D55

Loire

Loire

D751

Savennières

Béhuard

D751

Abbaye St Maur

Chalonnes

corniche Angerine

Rochefort-sur-Loire

Brissac-Quincé

D751

Le Thoureil

La Guimonnière

Chemellier

Gennes

Layon

Thouarcé

N160

Chemillé

imperious. It commands attention by the sheer weight and power of its seventeen bastion towers, 40 to 50m high (once they were taller and capped by pepperpot roofs), linked by a double row of walls roughly pentagonal in shape. The curtain wall is more than a kilometre long. Gardens are planted out between inner and outer walls. Seventeen bastion towers, gigantic elephants' feet, splay outwards as though to grip the dark grey metamorphosed rock on which the castle was built. The same dark shale is the material of which the towers are made, their glowering monotony relieved by bands of white limestone. Much of Angers was built with this shale, and drew upon itself the epithet 'Black Angers'. The blue-grey slate of Angers has roofed countless châteaux and mansions, and a visit to the slate quarries makes an unusual excursion.

Part of the feudal castle still has a deep, broad dry moat where a herd of fallow deer lives. You enter the castle by the drawbridge over the moat from Promenade du Bout du Monde. Splendidly sited for its strategic needs in medieval times, its bastions protected the castle on the three sides away from the river. Its western flank was then washed by the Maine. Beyond the far side lay the hostile lands of the Dukes of Brittany, allies of the English.

In the third century AD, a continuous protective wall, 1,200m long, was built to hold back barbarian invasions. Fragments of it are lodged in the south wall of the cathedral's sacristy.

A wooden fortress erected by Foulques Nerra had stood on the site before St Louis (Louis IX of the Capetian dynasty) rebuilt it in stone between 1220 and 1240. Over the centuries, parts of the castle's interior have been demolished and rebuilt. The surviving wing of the fifteenth-century Logis Royal, the king's quarters put up by Louis II of Anjou, stands next to the chapel which his wife Yolande of Aragon had constructed of the white tufa stone used in the building of many châteaux in the Valley. Within the chapel, note the vaulting and the carved keystones which include a reproduction of the True Cross of Baugé.

In the Logis Royal are four fifteenth-century Flemish tapestries of the Passion. Perhaps the most delightful is *La Dame à l'Orgue*. A woman plays a portable organ; other elegant characters make music with her; a boy blows the bellows; another plays with a dog; a third appears to be swinging a cat by its tail.

More tapestries are exhibited in the Logis du Gouverneur, built in the eighteenth century, across the courtyard. These fifteenth- to eighteenth-century works are only modest introductions to the real masterpiece of the Château d'Angers, the tapestries or *tentures* of *The Apocalypse*. A special building, the Grande Galerie, houses the 100m long and 5m high tapestries. Once they were more than half as long again. A red velvet background throws into relief the figures which convey the passion and pathos inherent in the theme of sin and damnation which so absorbed the medieval mind. Commissioned by Louis I of Anjou, the tapestry was made in the Paris workshops of Nicolas Bataille between 1377 and 1380 from designs by Hennequin de Bruges which are in the Bibliothèque Nationale in Paris. Seventy-seven pieces survive, faded but majestic and poignant, a remarkable achievement of preservation in the light of their history. They were transported to Arles in Provence in 1400 for the wedding of Louis II to Yolande. Stored at Baugé in 1476 for four years, then bundled away in Angers cathedral for 300 years, they were displayed once a

Château d'Angers, a panel of the fourteenth-century tapestries of The Apocalypse

year. In 1782 the church tried to sell *The Apocalypse*. There were no offers. During the Revolution the tapestries were thrown into the streets. People helped themselves, and pieces did every conceivable duty from being used as horse-blankets to draught-stoppers. In 1843 the Bishop of Angers bought up for 300 francs all the remains he could trace (mostly off a rubbish dump). The maltreated tapestries were once again displayed only on feast days, to leave the cathedral for their present home in 1952.

You can walk round the tapestries in your own time, or you can use a tele-guide commentary in English, or you can follow the explanations of each scene which are posted in the window embrasures. Some critics have said that, marvellous though they are, the tapestries have lost some of their mysterious magnetism since coming to the Grande Galerie. For most visitors, however, the exhibition is clear and enlightening.

The tapestries of Angers are by no means exhausted; the city is a major centre of tapestries that can be seen by the public. Across the river is La Doutre (*d'outre* meaning 'beyond' and implying, many years ago, a socially inferior status) which is reached by the upstream bridge of Pont de la Haute Chaine. Ten tapestries are displayed in what was once the huge ward in the former Hospital of St John (Ancien Hôpital St Jean). They belong to an entirely different epoch from those of the *Apocalypse*, though they were inspired by Bataille's work. These ten panels, 80m long, were begun in 1957 by Jean Lurçat and completed in 1966. The collection is called *Le Chant du Monde* (The Song of the World). Lurçat, a humanist of our time, has used abstract symbols, riotous colours and patterns against a sombre black background to express his fears of the genocidal instinct in today's techno-civilisation. He makes this clear in the titles he gives to the first four panels: 'the great menace', 'the man of Hiroshima', 'the great charnel house', 'the end of everything' before he comes to more optimistic themes. The series is acknowledged as a great work of art by a man who revived the impetus to tapestry-making. Whether the moral messages and sentiments are anything more than muddy and confused will depend on the viewer's intuitive perceptions and identification with the humanistic philosophy of Lurçat's old age.

Whatever response you have to the tapestries, the old hospital itself is well worth looking over. It was founded in 1174 by Henry II as part of his penance for the assassination of Archbishop Becket of Canterbury. The medieval hospital ward where the Lurçats is huge, spacious and beautifully vaulted. At one end of it is all the attractive paraphernalia of a seventeenth-century pharmacy. In the hospital gardens are a few remnants of Angers' Gallo-Roman past, and behind the chapel is a wine museum.

This visit across the river is something of a digression. Although there are some other old buildings in La Doutre, the main sightseeing is confined to the east bank of the Maine. The cathedral of St Maurice is best approached by the rising steps of the Montée St Maurice which leads to the west front. A late Romanesque façade is surmounted by

Porch of Angers cathedral

two dissimilar towers separated by a third, put up in the sixteenth century. Christ seated in majesty with four Evangelists fills the tympanum. The way the cathedral was roofed is interesting. An earlier church on the site had burned down, but its outer walls were intact, and it was decided to use them to construct an exceptionally wide nave. The architect dealt with the problem of stress such a roof-span entailed by raising the keystone of the ogival arches 3m higher than those of the side and cross arches. This high pitch of the groin-vaulting was the first to be used, and so became known as the Angevin vaulting which prepared the way for the Gothic style. It took eighty years to build St Maurice. By the time they came to tackle the transept and choir enough experience and confidence had been gained for them to make the vaulting lighter and more elegant through the use of additional ribs to strengthen the arches.

More tapestries ('the wallpaper of the Middle Ages', they have been called) — from Aubusson — hang in the cathedral, but they are not easy to see. Stained-glass windows start in the twelfth century, and there are modern ones, too. The Treasury contains some interesting pieces; there is a Roman font used for baptising the dukes of Anjou, and a red porphyry urn which had belonged to King René.

A little to the south of the cathedral is the Logis Barrault, facing the Jardin des Beaux-Arts. In this fine fifteenth-century Renaissance building is the Fine Arts Museum (Musée des Beaux-Arts). From the point of view of local art, the main attraction is a collection of plaster casts by the sculptor and medallionist, David d'Angers (1788-1856), son of a woodcarver of Angers. The house where he was born, 38 Rue David d'Angers, is marked with a plaque. Near the château

is a statue of Roi René by him, and a marble statue of Ste Cécile (actually the face of the lady who refused to marry David) behind the high altar of the cathedral. In the museum are statues and busts of many famous people of his day — Paganini, Goethe, Victor Hugo, Balzac among them. That this is a good provincial museum is underlined by the diversity of paintings from various schools; Fragonard, Watteau, Boucher, Corot, Chardin, Mignard, van Loo, Greuze, Ingres, to mention only some representatives of the French School.

Just west of Logis Barrault in a garden are the romantic ruins of Chapelle Toussaint, accidentally blown up in 1815 when the place was being used as a military arsenal. In the opposite direction, east of the Logis, is a thick-walled square keep, Tour St Aubin, which had been both bell-tower and place of refuge for the monks of the twelfth-century Abbaye St Aubin which lay at a little distance from the tower. Rebuilt in the seventeenth century, the abbey is now part of the Préfecture. During office hours, you can go in and see the remarkable carved rounded arcades of a Romanesque cloister and chapterhouse doorway which came to light in 1836. Best preserved of these stone carvings are those depicting David and Goliath, the latter being felled wearing a coat of Norman armour; in another scene his head is presented to Saul. Below, thirteenth-century frescoes in a fine state of preservation, tell the story of the Magi.

Still in the old town is Hôtel Pincé, just beyond Place du Ralliement. A graceful Renaissance building, it houses the Turpin de Crissé museum of Greek and Etruscan vases, *objets d'art* from China and Japan, sixteenth-century painted enamels, and engravings of the history of fashion in France.

Behind the Post Office is the

Château with Logis Royal, chapel, Logis du Gouverneur, *Apocalypse* tapestries.

Cathedral of St Maurice, stained-glass windows, treasury.

Tour St Aubin.

Logis Barrault and **Musée des Beaux-Arts**, sculpture of David d'Angers, paintings.

Ruins of one-time abbey-church of **Toussaint**.

Préfecture and Romanesque arcades, carvings, thirteenth-century frescoes.

Hôtel Pincé, Musée Turpin de Crissé. Fifteenth- to eighteenth-century houses in old quarters.

Ancien Hôpital St Jean, Musée Lurçat tapestries *Le Chant du Monde*, seventeenth-century pharmacy.

Eglise St Serge, best example of chancel vaulting in Angevin style, stained glass.

Collégiale St Martin, intact Carolingian building, Gallo-Roman and Merovingian remains in crypt.

Eglise de la Trinité, twelfth century, sixteenth-century belfry, bronze statuette of Notre Dame de Ronceray.

Ancienne Abbaye St Nicolas, reconstructed in eighteenth century.

Chapelle de la Barre, series of polychrome religious statues, exemplifying regional *terra cotta* work in seventeenth century.

Parc Municipal de la Garenne, Rue Chef de Ville, formed out of one-time garden of monks at Abbaye St Nicolas, views of Brionneau valley and St Nicolas lake.

Jardin des Plantes and **Arboretum de la Maulévrie**, exotic trees.

Collégiale St Martin. Built on the site of an early Christian cemetery which can be seen with its sarcophagi in the crypt, the collegiate church is something of a rarity for it is a largely intact Carolingian building of the ninth century. It was founded by none other than Foulques Nerra in one of his occasional moods of repentance and benevolence.

Here and there, when you stroll about the narrow streets or *ruelles* of the old quarters, you come across delightful examples of fifteenth- to eighteenth-century merchants' houses. One such is Maison d'Adam, Place Ste Croix, a fifteenth-century half-timbered house with five overhanging storeys and diamond-shaped lattices over the façades. Its timbers are covered with secular carvings. See also Hôtel du Croissant in Rue St Aignan.

North of Angers, and as far as Château-Gontier, a minor road more or less follows the east bank of the Mayenne and offers quiet and pleasant riverside villages to stop at: Angers, Feneu, Grez-Neuville, Chenillé-Changé, Marigne, Daon, Ménil (a little car ferry crosses the Mayenne here),

1 N23 west — Serrant (17km); outstanding Anjou château, sixteenth to eighteenth centuries, moat, park, gardens, sumptuously furnished, chapel and sculptures — St Georges-sur-Loire (1km) — left on D961 — cross Loire — Chalonnes (7km); attractive riverside town — left on D751 *Corniche Angevine* winding road cut in granite cliffs, extensive views — Rochefort-sur-Loire (9km); on Louet, old turreted houses, restored Romanesque church — D54 south — La Guimonnière château (4km); taste and buy Quarts de Chaume, best sweet Coteaux du Layon wine — return to Rochefort (4km) — over cross-roads on D106 — Ile de Béhuard (3km); in middle of Loire, large, inhabited, picturesque island, tiny church of Notre Dame partly in rock, statue, stained glass, fifteenth- to seventeenth-century houses in village — cross Loire — La Savennières (0.5km); (name derived from *Saponaria*, soapwort, plant once used locally for cleaning woollens and tapestries), taste and buy Coulée de Serrant wine at Château de la Roche-aux-Moines, steepest vineyard of Loire — D111 — Epiré — La Pointe — Bouchemaine on Loire — Prupiers along Maine — Angers (15.5km).

2 Boat excursions along Mayenne, Sarthe and Loir.

3 Angers — Ponts-de-Cé — cross Louet — left on D132 — Juignes-sur-Loire — Le Bois-Brainson (18km) — left on D55 — Abbaye St Maur (8km); restored Benedictine abbey — D132 riverside road — Le Thoureil (5.5km); one-time port for despatch of fruit, delightful village backed by orchards and vines — Gennes (4.5km); ruined church (views), twelfth-century tower with amusing carvings — D751 (Angers road) — menhir on left (0.5km) — another in 1.5km — left after La Genaudière on D90 — Chemellier (7.5km) — right fork on D123 — Brissac-Quincé (6km); impressive château, park, furnishings, tapestries — on Angers road, windmill Moulin du Grand Pavé, taste and buy Coteaux de l'Aubance wines — Angers (16km).

4 D952 east — left at La Pyramide (6km); erected in 1743 to commemorate completion of levee to halt flooding by Loire — Vissoire — Trélazé (2km) — St Barthélemy-d'Anjou (3.5km); clean, pleasant villages at heart of slate quarries (*ardoiseries*) 5km in extent. Known to have been mined in twelfth century, if not earlier, quarries supply high quality material for 75 per cent of France's slate roofs from modern shafts nearly 400m deep. Surrounding fields enclosed by unmortared slate walls. Disued quarries now being 'landscaped' by trees and vegetation — Château de Pignerolle; elegant late eighteenth century, Polish Government-in-exile HQ, 1939, German army HQ from 1940 — Angers (6km).

Serrant, one of the finest châteaux in Anjou

Coudray, Château-Gontier (about 63km).

Château-Gontier is an important cattle-market divided by the Mayenne. Narrow, irregular streets and riverside quays make the old town picturesque. In the Romanesque church of St Jean are frescoes; from the terraces behind are pleasant river views. There is also a museum with paintings, sculptures and antiquities.

Le Lion d'Angers (not connected with a lion but from the Latin *legio*, indicating a military base) is a little west of our road, and lies on the river Oudon. Just outside is the national stud and racecourse at Château l'Isle-Briand.

To one side or the other of the Angers to Château-Gontier road are a number of minor châteaux which entail only small deviations. They are diverse in style and period. For example, to the west of the river Mayenne are Le Plessis-

Macé, in the twelfth century a fortress against hostile Brittany; its fifteenth-century buildings are much restored Flamboyant Gothic; the spacious interior is furnished. Bois-Mautboucher, southwest of Chambellay, stands by a large lake; dating from the fifteenth and seventeenth centuries, furnished and with a picture gallery, it has been restored. Percher, 8.5km north of Le Lion d'Angers on the Château-Gontier road, is in mixed Gothic and Renaissance styles. Magnanne, southwest of Ménil, is in the formal style of Louis XIV, built of brick, and has fine interior woodwork, furniture and paintings. St Ouen at Chemazé, is an early sixteenth-century building of white tufa, richly decorated; there is also a simple chapel and house.

To the east of the Mayenne is the important Le Plessis-Bourré. Set in level ground with a wide moat and bridge, the

53

Le Plessis-Bourré, an impressive fifteenth-century building

fifteenth-century building has white walls, blue-grey slate roofs, pepperpot towers, interior courtyard, arcaded galleries. The interior is impressive, too, especially the guard-room with a coffered ceiling painted in the fifteenth century with amusing and sometimes rude allegorical figures. Northeast of Daon is the sixteenth-century fortified farmhouse of Manoir de l'Escoublère, flanked by four round towers, and enclosing a courtyard and well.

2 Valley of the Loir

A quietly meandering river is the Loir. It rises, 200 metres up, west of Chartres, flows south through Illiers-Combray (where Marcel Proust spent his childhood and later wove Combray into his immortal *A la Recherche du temps perdu*), through Châteaudun to Vendôme. By the time it joins the Sarthe and Mayenne above Angers after 350km it has descended 180 metres, to make it a peaceful, meadow-accompanied river which has cut small chalk embankments. It is a more intimate, small-scale Loire. It, too, is useless now to commerce; pleasure boats and fishermen have the stream to themselves.

Northeast from Angers N23 is the direct road to Seiches and La Flèche. A quieter way to Seiches is to leave N23 5.5km out of Angers for D52 which makes for Villevêque where tools of 400,000 years ago have been found. Cross the Loir, pass a dolmen on the right before coming to the agreeable little market-town of Seiches on the left bank. Beyond Matheflon is Château du Verger, or rather, the servants' quarters of what had once been perhaps the biggest and finest château anywhere in the valley. Why it was pulled down by Cardinal de Rohan in the eighteenth century is a mystery. An ancestor had built it 300 years earlier to receive kings and queens in fullest splendour.

Make a little detour to the village of Huillé which has a few delightful sixteenth- and seventeenth-century houses to show, before going to Durtal on the main road. Only the courtyard of Durtal's château can be visited. Porte Véron is what is left of the eleventh-century ramparts. To the south is the extensive Forêt de Chambiers of oaks, maritime pines, a stream, lakes and footpaths.

Traffic roars through the narrow main road of Bazouges but there is a free car park under the trees outside the church which is the chief reason for stopping. From the outside, thick simple walls show its twelfth-century origin. Inside, the wooden vaults were painted in the fifteenth century. Close to the Loir is a sixteenth-century château.

La Flèche, the last town on N23 for any of our itineraries, has a population of 16,500. 'A neat, clean little town', was Arthur Young's verdict in 1788. Why not spend a few days in this fruit-marketing centre, for it makes a good excursion centre?

In the late tenth century a castle was put up in the middle of the Loir. Rebuilt by the Carmelites in 1620, what is left now is part of the Hôtel de Ville. Charming river views are to be had from the middle of the bridge. Henri IV, most popular of any French king for the prosperity he strove to bring, for his courageous and amiable character, decreed that a place of learning be instituted in his Château Neuf at La Flèche by the Jesuits. The king had a strong attachment to the town. He was conceived there (although born at Pau) and spent much of his youth in Château Neuf. In 1603 the college was created. In its heyday fifteen hundred students worked there simultaneously. Most famous of its pupils was René Descartes (1596-1650) who profoundly influenced French thinking. Sweeping aside the

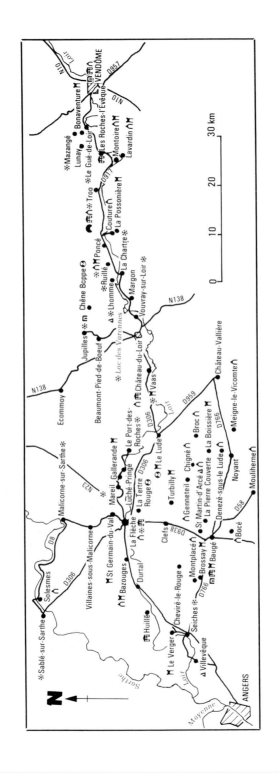

philosophical tenets of his day, he applied instead a mathematical approach to every aspect of knowledge. Some thinkers see in Cartesian philosophy the source of all modern philosophy's errors. His logic certainly seems often to lead to a line of argument a non-Cartesian mind finds hard to follow.

When the Jesuits were expelled in 1762, the college was converted to a preparatory school for the Ecole Militaire in Paris. The Revolution shut it down. In 1808 Napoleon reopened it as the *Prytanée Impérial Militaire*. So uncouth were the manners of its pupils that they were nicknamed *'Brutions'*. *Prytanée* derives from the Greek but its meaning was distorted by the Revolution to signify an institution where sons of officers received a free education so as to enter a *Grande Ecole*. Its purpose today is similar. The entrance arch in Rue du Collège is surmounted by a bust of Henri IV; an urn in the seventeenth-century Chapelle St Louis is said to contain the ashes of his heart and those of his wife, Marie de Médici.

Take a look also at the little Romanesque Chapelle Notre Dame-des-Vertus which contains woodcarvings brought from Château du Verger outside Seiches.

One popular excursion is to the zoo at La Tertre-Rouge, 5km south on D104. In pine woods which cover eighteen acres are various mammals, from monkeys to elephants, birds — especially birds of prey — reptiles and snakes in vivaria. A museum illustrates with dioramas the region's wild life, the whole conceived by the naturalist, Jacques Bouillault.

In complete contrast — and in the opposite direction — is a visit to Solesmes Abbey, 28km away. Here, the magnet is the majestic and world famous

PLACES TO VISIT FROM LA FLÈCHE

Cheviré-le-Rouge
Twelfth-century church belfry and choir, eighteenth-century statues.

Montplacé
Twelfth-century wood *pietà*, seventeenth-century *terra cotta* Virgin and Child in chapel.

Brossay
Renaissance manor with octagonal towers.

Baugé
Château built by Yolande of Aragon on site of Foulques Nerra castle, now *Mairie*, remarkable staircase; old mansions; Hospice St Joseph, one of finest seventeenth-century pharmacies in France, collection of decorated jars; sixteenth-century chapel with large double-armed fragment of True Cross encrusted with gold and precious stones.

Gregorian chant sung by the Benedictine monks. Mass can be attended every morning and Vespers every evening.

On the way to Solesmes call at Sablé-sur-Sarthe. It is a delightful starting-point for river excursions. Take a longer way back to La Flèche by following the Sarthe to Malicorne (there are pottery works just east of the village). Then take the lanes south through Villaines-sous-Malicorne and St Germain-du-Val where David Hume lived from 1734 in Château d'Yvandeau while writing his chief philosophical work, *Treatise of Human Nature*.

East from La Flèche is a very pleasant run through Mareil-sur-Loir, past the fifteenth-century château de Gallerande

Solesmes Abbey, famous for Georgian chant sung by Benedictine monks, overlooking River Sarthe

on the left, through Pringé to Luché-Pringé, turning right beyond the village. This little rural ride takes you through luscious riverside vegetation to Le Port-des-Roches (you might be tempted to stay a day or two at the small hotel), and the drive can be continued at will through the sleepy countryside.

After La Flèche comes Le Lude on the D306. Le Lude puts on lavish *son-et-lumière* shows; full dramatic advantage is taken of château, river and gardens. The square château, a round tower at each corner, is of various eras and much restored. A diversity of period furnishings ornament the halls and rooms.

The D306 keeps as close as it can to the Loir. Vaas (*Vedacium* in Gallo-Roman days) has a well-arranged beach, and a medieval castle, captured and recaptured by French and English. Château-du-Loir's old town clusters

round Eglise St Guingalois. The D73B goes north to follow the pretty valley of the Yre to Beaumont-Pied-de-Boeuf (why this curious name?) and Jupilles surrounded by the Forêt de Bercé covering some 13,800 acres. The trees are mostly of common oak (exported throughout Europe), Spanish chestnut, maritime and Scots pine, and beech. Oaks are felled when they are between 200 and 240 years old. Guided tours of the Futaie des Clos start from the Chêne Boppe (named after a distinguished forestry expert), blasted by lightning in 1936. Forest tracks (*routes forestières*) lead to the sources of two streams, Fontaine de la Coudre and, further east, Source de l'Hermitière. At Jupilles you can visit the woodcraft museum, Musée du Bois.

Southeast of Forêt de Bercé is the riverside resort of La Chartre-sur-le-Loir surrounded by the Val du Loir vineyards: La Chartre, the other Vouvray, Marçon, Ruillé (Clos de Sous les Bois), Lhomme and its prestigious Clos des Janières. La Chartre is one of the *Stations Vertes de Vacances* whose amenities in the way of hotels, camp sites, swimming pool, tennis courts are set in rural surroundings. Days can be spent ambling about the tranquil countryside, visiting churches, manor houses, vineyards, Lac des Varennes, Pierre Maupertuis dolmen at Lhomme. At Poncé, the sixteenth century château, restored some sixty years ago, stands at the foot of a chalk cliff. The tall building possesses a Renaissance staircase of six straight flights in parallel. They pass through coffered vaults decorated with innumerable mythological sculptures. In the formal garden is a large pigeon-loft, complete with turning ladders. A path clambers the cliff. At the top is a museum of local crafts and a studio where potters work and sell their products. At the western entrance to the village, at Moulin de Paillard by the river, are two workshops producing a wide range of artefacts. In Poncé church are some faded murals dating from 1170-80. One is a battle scene between

ROMANESQUE CHURCHES AROUND BAUGE

St Martin-d'Arcé; *La Pierre Couverte* dolmen; Clefs; Genneteil; Chigné; Broc; Denezé-sous-le-Lude; Meigné-le-Vicomte; Ancienne Abbaye de la Boissière; Pontigné; Bocé; Mouliherne (note light Angevin architecture); Château Turbilly (the 'Tourbilly' Arthur Young had utmost difficulty in finding during his agronomic researches in 1788; he had to hire a guide).

Saracens and Crusaders, a somewhat rare theme.

Upstream, turn right to Couture. Just short of the village is Manoir de la Possonnière, birthplace of the 'Prince of Poets', Pierre de Ronsard (1524-85). The rambling, unpretentious Renaissance house, with Latin and French inscriptions carved in stone, may not be visited; only the outside can be seen when the owners are absent. Some of the wine cellars were hewn out of the rock.

Château of Le Lude

Possonière comes from the word 'poinçon', a liquid measure which I take to be a 'puncheon' in English, a cask holding between 72 and 120 gallons, a suitable name for the wine-enjoying Ronsard household.

Ronsard became leader of a group of poets called *La Pléiade* which aimed to enrich the French language by imitating the masterpieces of classical antiquity, and creating elegant poetry for the élite of the court. In this aim he was joined by his friend Joachim du Bellay (1522-60), another Angevin poet, born at La Turmelière outside Liré not far from Nantes. Ronsard early became a page at court, and was in Scotland and England before returning to the court of France. Illness induced deafness, and he turned to writing the sonnets by which he is remembered. Successive kings patronised him; he was on friendly terms with Elizabeth I and Mary Queen of Scots. A prey to gout, he retired in 1572

to his priories of Ste Madeleine de Croixval (the ruins are outside Marcé) or Ste Cosme-de-Tours where he died. In Couture church where Ronsard was baptised, are the tombs of his parents. A commemorative plaque has been placed on l'Isle Verte where Ronsard wished to be buried. His poems sing sensuous praises to many corners: Vendôme, Troo, Croixval, Couture, Tours, Blois, Talcy, Bourgueil.

Troo is an unusual place. It sits atop a steep hill, its belfry visible from the valley. It can be written Troo or Trôo. The latter is a kind of pictorial image of the belfry roof, but Michelin prosaically leaves off the circumflex from its map. Narrow, stepped streets, bits of feudal walls, subterranean passages called *caforts*, make the little place labyrinthine and old. The impression is heightened by the remains of a medieval lazar-house, the Maladrerie Ste Catherine. From La Butte, the tumulus which offers a broad panorama, you can look down on chimneys of cave-dwellings beneath your feet. Along the valley you see signs pointing to *Habitations troglodytes* wherever there is a chalk cliff. Most are used for storing things but some, as at Troo, are inhabited. Up the hill is the Ancienne Collégiale St Martin, originally eleventh century and added to in later centuries. North of Troo is the Grand Puits, a deep and echoing well roofed over, while in Rue Basse is the Grotte Pétrifiante whose stalactites and petrified objects can be visited. On the other side of the river is the little church of St Jacques-de-Guérets whose fine twelfth-century murals of the Life of Christ have a Byzantine aspect. The most impressive is the large *Descent into Hell*.

Both Troo and Montoire, seven kilometres away, were stations on the pilgrimage routes to St James of Compostela in Spain and to the tomb of

Twelfth-century fresco in Chapelle St Gilles, Montoire

Ruins of Lavardin castle besieged by Henry II and Richard Coeur-de-Lion in 1188

St Martin in Tours which is why both had lazar-houses. Other than the views, the ruined keep at Montoire holds little interest. The pleasantest sight is from the bridge over the Loir: placid water, weeping willows, old house-fronts, boats, fishermen. Chapelle St Gilles, once part of a Benedictine priory of which Ronsard had been the titular head, also has twelfth and thirteenth century frescoes. Again, a Byzantine influence appears in the postures, shape of eyes, the rays of light streaming from Christ's hands on to the heads of the Apostles.

Across the river is the romantic ruin of the eleventh century castle of Lavardin, seated on a chalk promontory. Three concentric rings of defensive walls enclosed some twelve acres. The square keep still stands, as do remains of towers and defence works round the drawbridge, and some vaults of later buildings. Henry II of England and his son Richard Coeur-de-Lion laid unsuccessful siege to Lavardin in 1188. In 1448 the Treaty of Lavardin was signed here between Charles VII and the English.

Yet more wall-paintings (some frescoes, others distemper) are in the church of St Genest in Lavardin's Grande Rue. In this very early, archaic Romanesque building are particularly well preserved twelfth- to sixteenth-century works which were brought to light in 1914. In Rue de la Barrière some fifteenth-century half-timbered houses have survived.

Most publicised of all troglodyte

61

houses are those at Les Roches-l'Evêque on the road to Vendôme. Beflowered doors and windows front the houses built entirely in the warm chalk cliff. Chapelle St Nicolas (twelfth century), on the Vendôme road, was once another lazar-house. Lunay, 4km beyond Les Roches-l'Evêque, has a large church with frescoes (fourteenth and fifteenth centuries).

A little detour after Lunay takes you to the attractive village of Mazangé, then past the Manoir de Bonaventure (associated with the family of the poet Alfred de Musset), to Le Gué-du-Loir, a pretty spot where the Boulon stream flows into the Loir.

From here, past Villiers church (sixteenth-century wall paintings), you come to Vendôme by pleasant minor roads, a town of over 18,000 inhabitants. Gaulish village, then *Vindocinum* (whose Gallo-Roman remains were excavated 2km upstream); pillaged by the English in 1361; inherited by the Bourbons; the place where Baboeuf, a petty official who led a small primitive communist group against the revolutionary Directory, was put to death in 1797; where the novelist Balzac had a miserable schooling at what is now the Lycée Ronsard, on the site of the poet's house; scene of a battle in the Franco-Prussian War of 1870; damaged by Italian aircraft in 1940.

Once the outlying sprawl has been penetrated, the old town has a number of buildings which repay a visit. In Place St Martin stands the fifteenth-century Cloche St Martin, the only remnant of a church destroyed in 1856. In a row of old mansions, Hôtel du Saillant (fifteenth century) was owned by the du Bellay family, later to become the infirmary of the school whose rigid discipline Balzac so much hated. *La Montagne* is the rather elevated name given to the high ground on which the château stands. From it, you can return to the heart of Vendôme by Faubourg St Lubin which crosses the river under the handsome Renaissance Porte St Georges.

The chief attraction is the one-time Abbaye de la Trinité and its free-standing twelfth century belfry, square at the base, ending in an octagon supporting a spire and a cross, 80m high.

Stained glass, statuary and carved misericord choir-stalls (the subjects carved are non-scriptural because, as an indulgence, the priest's bottom was permitted to rest on these seats during the drawn-out offices of medieval times) are in the church. Attached to the conventual buildings is a museum which concentrates on religious and artisanal work of the region as well as on its local archaeology.

From Vendôme the Loir takes a northward course, and pleasant minor roads follow it.

Vendôme, Abbaye de la Trinité and twelfth-century belfry

3 Saumur and the Vienne

Saumur retains an air of old-world provincialism. When it was a Protestant stronghold its population was larger than today's until the Revocation of the Edict of Nantes in 1685 when thousands fled the town. Atmosphere, history, food and wine make Saumur (literally 'safe wall') appealing to the visitor. Buildings constructed out of the local white tufa rock catch the eye, as do the Angers roof-slates. Saumur's strategic position has ensured a political and commercial importance greater than its actual size.

Most of the town lies south of the Loire. On the elongated island — once known as l'Ile d'Or — fishermen lived in almost total autonomy in King René's time. There is parking along the quays (where weekend market stalls add vitality to the scene), near the château and elsewhere in the town centre. Hotels and restaurants are modestly priced.

Tufa becomes whiter with age, and so the old château is a white icing-sugar fortress. Best first impressions are from across the river; you see it high on its *butte* (once lined with windmills) over the town. Four-sided but irregularly shaped, it is supported by four machicolated pepper-pot towers. From the battlements the Loire spreads far on either side. Inside are two outstanding, specialist museums. One is the Museum of Decorative Arts displaying highest

---

WHAT TO SEE IN SAUMUR

Château, Avenue du Dr Petou: Musée des Arts Décoratifs; Musée du Cheval.
Eglise Notre Dame-de-Nantilly, Rue de Nantilly: oldest church in Saumur (twelfth century, Flamboyant Gothic additions); fifteenth- and eighteenth-century tapestries; twelfth-century painted wooden statue of Notre Dame-de-Nantilly; carved epitaph to King René's wet-nurse Tiphaine (1458).
Eglise St Pierre, Rue Dacier: sixteenth-century tapestries; Baroque organ-loft; Angevin vaulting.
Jardin des Plantes: series of vine-bedecked terraces.
Musée de la Cavalerie, Avenue Foch: history of cavalry and armour.
Horses and tanks on display by Ecole de l'Armée Blindée et de la Cavalerie for four days, end July (*Grand Carrousel*). Cavalry School founded by Louis XV.
Hôtel de Ville: restored, parapets etc. once part of town's defensive walls; fifteenth-century fireplaces.
Chapelle St Jean, behind Town Hall: early thirteenth century, Angevin style.
Notre Dame-des-Ardilliers, Quai L. Mayaud: seventeenth century; once major pilgrimage centre.
Old town: between Quais and Château; small medieval streets, shops, new buildings in old style to create harmonious unity.
Grand Dolmen de Bagneux, Rue du Dolmen: 17.5m long, covered by four capstones.

Ussé Château

Chenonceaux Château

Château of Blois

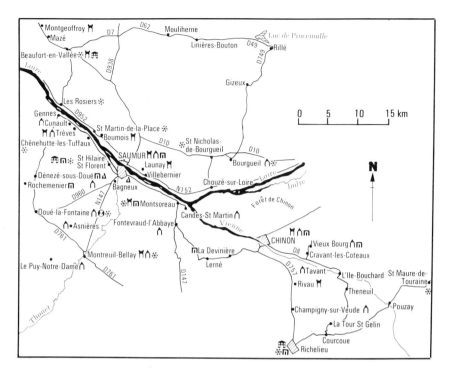

quality china from many parts of
Europe, as well as paintings, tapestries,
furniture, carved wooden statuettes. The
other, the Horse Museum, traces the
history of the horse from the earliest
times.

Saumur sparkling wine is made in the
western suburb of St Hilaire-St Florent.
A long street of *salons de dégustation*
allows you to taste and buy. Look out
for *Appellation Crémant de Loire*,
probably the best. Chalk cliffs are also
exploited for mushroom growing, and
Musée du Champignon shows how
different varieties of commercial
mushrooms are grown. Almost next
door a guide shows you round the Ecole
Nationale d'Equitation's modern stables
for 120 horses.

The next village, Chênehutte-les-
Tuffaux holds an annual Mushroom
Fair in early May. This picturesque road
shows off the Loire to best advantage.

*Floodlit Saumur château from across the
Loire*

Continue along it to Trèves ('Truce', a name invented with sardonic humour by Foulques Nerra for his castle here), a tiny village with a squat Romanesque church cowering beneath a round fifteenth-century keep. Cunault's Romanesque church is finely proportioned and carved.

On to Gennes (dealt with in Chapter 1). Turn left on the D69 to Dénezé-sous-Doué. Its oddity is the *Caverne Sculptée*, a cave whose walls are sculpted with hundreds of grotesque figures, thought to have been executed in the sixteenth century by a secret society of sculptors; these strange effigies were part of the initiation rite. Still older, but more orthodox, is the eleventh- and twelfth-century church. Under its wooden porch are graffiti by soldiers in Year II of the Revolutionary calendar (1793-4).

At the village of Rochemenier (off the D69 and west along the D177 for 1km) is a remarkable underground Peasant Museum. Until the 1930s, the whole village occupied chalk caves (*caves demeurantes*), and the museum, consisting of two erstwhile farms, shows how troglodytic peasants lived and worked. A similar subterranean museum is at La Fosse (take the D177 for 5km, then right), save that this one is occupied by a family and animals, a living example of an unusual bygone way of life.

Doué-la-Fontaine is a mixture of broad, modern streets and an old town built on the pitted chalk plateau. Below ground are caves, some still used for storage, but most have been abandoned. Doué is best known for its nurseries and rose-gardens. The *Jardin des Roses* is on Route de Soulanger. In mid-July is the annual Rose Festival (*Journées des Roses*) held in the open quarries which the Romans may have worked in the

Trèves, fifteenth-century keep

Market day in front of the château at Montreuil-Bellay

suburb of Douce. The arena is used for theatre and music shows. Beneath are cavernous vaults where whole communities once lived. Another attraction is the *Parc Zoologique des Minières*, Route de Cholet. In ten acres of one-time quarries live a variety of mammals and birds.

The D761 goes straight to Montreuil-Bellay on the banks of the Thouet. Half way along the road a short detour to the left brings you to the ruins of Abbaye d'Asnières whose chancel is a lovely example of Angevin Gothic, and there are some charming stone carvings of the fourteenth century in the abbot's chapel and oratory.

Montreuil-Bellay is in a most picturesque setting: gardens by the river dotted with islets and spanned by a

Montreuil-Bellay, Porte de Ville

bridge, an old water-mill, a ruined twelfth-century church, the castle, a fifteenth-century church, sections of medieval walls and two gatehouses. The present château, built in the fifteenth century, had cannon-balls rather than archers in mind. The thirteen flanking towers had flat roofs from which artillery could be fired. You are shown the medieval kitchens, wine-press, bath rooms, circular stairways leading to four suites in the Petit-Château, the seigneurial chapel, much restored, within the castle walls.

Another splendid example of Angevin Gothic architecture is at Le Puy-Notre-Dame on a high mound 7.5km west of Montreuil-Bellay. A treasure of the church is a bejewelled Girdle of Our Lady brought from Jerusalem.

Follow the south bank of the Loire upstream past Dampierre and Souzay, where a large island has created a secondary channel. Local vineyards produce Champigny wines. All the villages hereabouts have interesting churches. Montsoreau, an agreeable town and a beach of sand, has a fifteenth-century château, part fortress, part country seat, with lovely views of Loire, Vienne and vineyards. Its Musée des Goums deals with the French conquest of Morocco.

Just south is Moulin de la Herpinière, originally a fifteenth-century windmill whose grindstone was lodged underground, and now an artists' workshop open to the public.

Next door to Montsoreau is Candes-St Martin just in Touraine, where the Vienne enters the Loire. The church marks the spot where St Martin, the apostle of Christianity in Touraine, died in 397. His recumbent statue lies in the church whose Angevin architecture gives it a soaring aspect.

Fontevraud-l'Abbaye, just in Anjou, draws thousands of visitors. Founded in

Fontevraud-l'Abbaye, effigy of Richard I, Richard Coeur-de-Lion

the eleventh century, the monastery quickly comprised five separate buildings: for monks, nuns, lepers, other sick persons, and repentant women. In its heyday, 5,000 people were housed, always under the authority of an abbess, usually an aristocrat. Patronised by the Counts of Anjou they chose, as kings of England, to be buried at Fontevraud: Henry II, his wife Eleanor of Aquitaine, their son Richard I, Isabella of Angoulême, wife of Richard's brother John Lackland. Their painted effigies remain intact, for all the desecration wrought by Huguenots in 1562, Revolutionaries in 1793 who jumbled all the bones together, and Napoleon who turned the place into a prison in 1804, which it remained until 1963. Now it has been restored.

Fontevrand-l'Abbaye, some of the twenty chimneys of the medieval kitchens

There is much to see in the church and conventual buildings, and the guided tour is a long one. The medieval kitchens are quite astonishing for their beauty and utility. From outside, a cluster of twenty pepper-pot chimneys connect with artfully placed flues which extracted smoke from five fireplaces within.

A narrow road leads southeast to meet D117 where the left turn takes you through Lerné, then Seuilly and La Devinière, the probable birthplace of François Rabelais (?1494-1553). This simple country house of his lawyer father is now a little museum. Much of his ribald youthful fantasy spilled into his *Gargantua* (1534) where all the place names of the district occur. One of the giant Gargantua's exploits takes place at Lerné. A quarrel arose between the *fouaciers* or cake-bakers of Lerné, subjects of King Picrochole, and the shepherds of Seuilly. This imagined king may have been drawn from a real figure, a physician to the nuns at Fontevraud and Lord of Lerné, who had been in legal dispute with Rabelais' father. The *fouaciers* of Lerné poured a stream of insults on the shepherds: 'shite-a-bed scoundrels, blockish grutnols, doddipol joltheads, jobbernol goosecaps' are only a few of the defamations which fill a huge paragraph.

But Rabelais the lawyer-monk-physician is more than effervescent scatology. His obscene buffooneries were intended to offend orthodox religious piety; his shafts were aimed at the abuses by the Catholic Church. As a Renaissance humanist, he accepted man and nature as they are, not as the theology of his day willed them to be. His orgies of gluttony let mortals revel in life; the swilling of wine is an ecstatic redemption through the wine of Christ's

69

blood, expressed by a satirical sixteenth-century pen.

From La Devinière, the short run to Chinon along the Vienne allows you to see from a distance the ruined château straddling its 400m long spur of rock. Its history is tied up with the Anglo-Angevin story. Henry II, who died at Chinon, built a part of the fortress, as did his son Richard I. Before visiting the château it may be as well to get a flavour of medieval Chinon by walking through the old parts north of the quays: along Rue Voltaire and Grand Carroi, Rue Hoche, Rue Jeanne d'Arc, Rue de la Lamproie (No 15 is the site of Rabelais' house) among others.

For a leisurely drive parallel to the Vienne, leave Chinon by the D8. Here and there you can make your way down to the clear and tranquil river's edge. Turn left where a signpost points across the vineyards to Cravant-les-Côteaux. Just beyond is Vieux Bourg, the nave of whose church (a small museum inside) is a rare example of early tenth-century Carolingian architecture. At l'Ile-Bouchard cross the river. To see the little Romanesque church of St Nicolas at Tavant, follow the D760 west for two kilometres and look out for a sharp and narrow entrance to the lane which leads to the church. It holds twelfth-century frescoes of an originality almost unique in France.

Or else make for Richelieu. By the direct road (D757) it is 16km. On the way is Château du Rivau (fifteenth century) visited by Joan of Arc to replenish her team-horses; it is richly

WHAT TO SEE IN CHINON

Château
Fort St Georges (dismantled);
Château du Milieu (Joan of Arc
Museum); Fort du Coudray; Logis
Royaux; *son-et-lumière*.

Eglise St Mexme
Tenth-century nave; two towers;
large fifteenth-century frescoes.

Chapelle Ste Radegonde
Twelfth century, built in rock;
frescoes of Plantagenet kings on
horseback discovered 1964;
troglodyte houses.

Eglise St Etienne
Reconstructed in fifteenth century;
fine Flamboyant façade.

Eglise St Maurice
Built by Henry II; Romanesque nave
and tower. Joan of Arc prayed here;
her statue and image in modern
stained-glass windows.

Statue of Rabelais
Place de l'Hôtel-de-Ville.

Medieval Market
Takes place on first weekend each
August.

Jardin Anglais
Along river Vienne.

Musée du Vin
Rue du Dr Gendron; in caves.

Caves Peintes
Rue des Caves Peintes; underground
galleries below château where
Rabelais drank 'many glasses of good
fresh wine', his model for *Cave de la
Dive Bouteille* in *Gargantua*.

Musée du Vieux Chinon
Rue Haute St Maurice; local arts and
traditions; portrait of Rabelais by
Delacroix (1834).

*Elegant eighteenth-
century Château de
Montgeoffroy*

Lively twelfth-century frescoes in church of St Nicholas, Tavant

furnished. Champigny-sur-Veude has a beautiful Renaissance church. By prettier lanes through Theneuil, Chezelles, La Tour-St Gelin, Courcoue, it is 18km.

Richelieu, with a population of 2,500, was laid out in the seventeenth century in a rectangle, 700m by 500m, its buildings in Neo-classical style, an example of town-planning. Once

---

A Tour North of Saumur

Saumur — left on D229 — Château de Boumois (on lane on right, fifteenth-century Flamboyant Gothic in white tufa; dovecote with revolving ladder; mementoes of naval family of Dupetit-Thouars) — join D952 — St Martin-de-la-Place (riverside views) — Les Rosiers (suspension bridge; thirteenth-century church; old houses) — D59 — Beaufort-en-Villée (spring and autumn flowers grown for seed-merchants; seventeenth century mansions; ruined castle; views) — left on N147, right on D74 — Mazé — Montgeoffroy (simple, elegant eighteenth-century château; fine original furniture) — Beaufort

— D7 — La Croix-de-Bois-Maudet — D62 — Mouliherne — Linières-Bouton (Lac de Pincemalle) — D49 — Rillé — D749 — Gizeux — Bourgueil (note espalier-trained vines in vicinity; church; covered market; abbey) — D35 — St Nicolas-de-Bourgueil (vineyards) — left — Chouzé-sur-Loire — right on N152 — river views — Villebernier — right — Launay (Manoir de Launay built by King René; pretty white stone and pepper-pot slated roof; viewed only through gates) — Villebernier — Saumur.

Total distance 115km.

Bourgueil, the famous vineyards

moated, gardens now surround it. Twenty-eight identical, handsome houses line the Grande Rue. In Place du Marché is a splendidly raftered covered market. A little museum is in the Hôtel de Ville. Of Cardinal Richelieu's château little remains other than the impressive park.

If you return to the river Vienne at Pouzay, continue to Ste Maure-de-Touraine in goats' cheese country, to see a handsome medieval covered market restored in 1672.

4 Tours and its Countryside

Tours wears the air of a capital city. Religious capital when St Martin evangelised Touraine; intellectual capital with the presence of Gregory of Tours and Alcuin of York; political capital for Gauls, Romans, the province of Touraine; a more temporary one for the hopeless organisation of resistance to the Germans in 1870, again in 1940. A university centre since 1970, and a musical one with its *Fêtes Musicales de Touraine* since 1964.

Its ambitious expansion makes its outlying sprawl as unlikeable as the cementscapes of any other growing town. Persist and penetrate to its stimulating heart. The old part feels human. What war destroyed in 1940 and 1944 has been thoughtfully rebuilt. With your own car you can radiate from Tours, or else you can use the local tourist facilities such as coach tours to châteaux or river trips. At the Tourist Office individual audio equipment can be hired for a tour of the old city with tapes in English. Accommodation ranges from Hôtel Méridien which has tennis courts and private swimming pool to modest but quite adequate bed-and-breakfast places in both the centre and suburbs. At a rought estimate Tours has some 250 restaurants; at most the standard is very high, say the gourmets. Restaurant Barrier heads the list by reputation and price, but under the same ownership is La Petite Marmite at a fifth of the Barrier's price. Outdoor cafés overlooking the river are plentiful.

There is a public swimming pool, golf, tennis courts, some twenty riding schools, fishing, water-sports, cycling, rambling. At St Avertin is an extensive leisure centre. Public gardens are dotted about the town; Jardin des Prébendes-d'Oé, Rue Salengro, covers ten acres of flowers and shady trees.

Most of what will interest the visitor lies south of the Loire and north of the Cher, 3km distant. The north-south artery is Rue Nationale carried over the Loire by one of France's loveliest eighteenth-century stone bridges, the Pont Wilson, *le Pont de Pierre*, as locals mostly speak of it. Rue Nationale becomes Avenue de Grammont at Place Jean Jaurès out of which lead, to the east, Boulevard Heurteloup (leading to Place Maréchal Leclerc where Tourist Office, coach and railway stations are), and west, Boulevard Béranger. Smart shops are in Rue Nationale and Rue Bordeaux. Nearer the Loire, Rue Colbert goes east from Rue Nationale, and is with Rue de la Scellerie full of intriguing small shops of every sort. No 41 Rue Colbert, a gabled house, has a metal sign hanging outside. It is Joan of Arc in armour; below is written *A la Pucelle Armée* ('To the Maiden Army'). To the house which previously occupied the site Joan came to have a suit of armour fitted while a Scotsman, Hamish Power, living in Tours, painted her standard.

Turn right out of Rue Colbert to reach the cathedral of St Gatien. It took from the thirteenth to the sixteenth centuries to build; the result is a harmonious mixture of Gothic, Flamboyant and Renaissance styles. Stained-glass windows flood the interior with glowing light. You can go to the top of the south

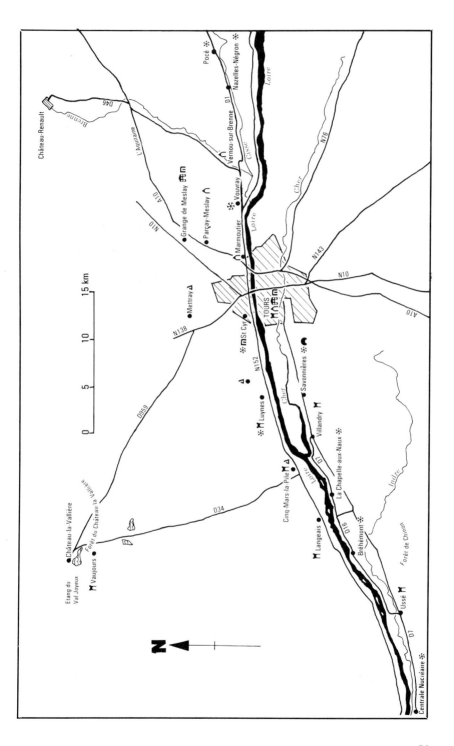

tower. Next door is the choir-school, La Psalette, another elegant construction of the fifteenth and sixteenth centuries.

To the north is what remains of Henry II's Château Royal de Tours. Two twelfth-century towers still stand; within is an historical waxwork museum. South of the cathedral is the Musée des Beaux-Arts in the former palace of the archbishop. Near the entrance is a small round tower, a late Gallo-Roman fragment of the defence walls of *Caesarodunum*. Scattered at random round the halls of the museum are some important paintings: Rubens, Rembrandt, two Mantegnas, Jean Fouquet (a native of Tours); later artists such as Degas, Delacroix, Nattier; and sculptors including Bourdelle, Houdon and the local Sicard. Some rooms are decorated with Tours silks which, in the fifteenth and sixteenth centuries were turned out from some of the 2,000 looms which employed 20,000 workers.

Retrace Rue Colbert to find on your right the picturesque Place Foire-le-Roi. Medieval food markets were held here under the protection of the king. Trestles were converted into a stage for the presentation of open-air mystery plays. One of the old houses in Rue Colbert is Hôtel Babou de la Bourdaisière (No 8) of 1520, in whose courtyard are three fourteenth-century arches transferred from the Augustinian cloisters. Eglise St Julien, founded by Gregory of Tours, still retains fragments from the eleventh-century building; the rest dates from the twelfth and thirteenth centuries, but the stained-glass windows are modern. Following the bombing of 1940, the church cellars were rediscovered. Now the great vaults are hosts to a splendidly catholic Musée des Vins de Touraine. Not only is it a history of wine-making, but also of the relationship between wine and human societies.

No less fascinating is the Musée du

Cathedral of St Gatien, Tours

Compagnonnage, entered at 8 Rue Nationale, a history of craft guilds from the fifteenth century on. Tools and fine examples of work in different trades are on show. Documents are displayed which relate to the nationwide organisation which, persecuted by larger existing unions, met in secret and evolved rituals which the Freemasons may have borrowed later on. It is worth coming to Tours just to see these two illuminating exhibitions, both the brain-child of one man.

Entered by a porch at 28 Rue Nationale is the Jardin de Beaune-Semblançay, with a finely carved fountain (1511) in front of the *hôtel's* façade and gallery.

76

1 Place Plumereau (fifteenth-century houses) — Rue Briçonnet (No 35, twelfth-century house, among others) — Rue du Mûrier (Hôtel Rimbaud, 1825, contains Musée du Gemmail, showing modern techniques of using coloured glass particles in relief and illuminated from within), and other *hôtels* of different periods; No 16, Hôtel de Pierre du Puy (fifteenth century), occupied by *Centre d'Etudes de Langues Vivantes* (Centre for Studies of Living Languages) — Rue des Tanneurs (university buildings on left) — Rue Littré — Eglise St Saturnin (1473) — Rue des Carmes — Rue Paul-Louis Courier, more old houses of great diversity: No 18, Hôtel Bihet (fifteenth century, wooden spiral staircase in courtyard supported by wooden arches leading to gallery) — Rue du Commerce — Place St Pierre-le-Puellier (gardens, Gallo-Roman and medieval cemetery; church foundations).

2 Place Plumereau — Rue du Grand-Marché — Place du Grand-Marché (picturesque alleyways in immediate vicinity) — Rue de Châteauneuf (No 13, Hôtel de Jean Briçonnet, fifteenth to sixteenth centuries) — Place de Châteauneuf — Rue des Halles — Tour de l'Horloge and Tour Charlemagne (restored) — Vestiges of eleventh to thirteenth century Basilica of St Martin — new Basilica of St Martin (nineteenth to twentieth century), grandly pompous, contains fragment of skull and tomb of St Martin, on his original fourth-century burial site).

Elegant Renaissance Hôtel Gouin, Tours, houses the archaeological museum

Prieuré de St Cosme
West of Tours in riverside suburb of
St Riche; eleventh and twelfth
centuries, mostly ruined; tomb of
Ronsard; twelfth-century refectory.

Château de Plessis-lès-Tours
A little south-east of St Cosme:
remains of Louis XI's fifteenth-
century château and souvenirs (he
died here in 1483).

Dolmen de Mettray
10km north-west by N138, right at La
Membrolle, through Mettray on St
Antoine-du-Rocher road, signposted
on right; huge dolmen, 5,000 years
old by stream.

Parçay-Meslay
10km by N10 and right; Romanesque
frescoes on church vaults.

Grange du Meslay
11km by N10; finest surviving
medieval tithe-barn surrounded by
fortified farm belonging to Abbey of
Marmoutier; Touraine music festival,
exhibitions.

Abbaye de Marmoutier
Rochecorbon, 5km east on N152;
founded by St Martin in 372, abbey
almost totally destroyed; present
building occupied by nuns who show
hillside caves where hermits lived.

St Cyr
West on N152, right at St Cyr *mairie*,
follow signposts to *La Béchellerie*;
home of Anatole France, 1914-24
where he died. Small museum in
memory of one of most stylish,
sceptical, pessimistic French writers.
Almost opposite, *La Gaudinière*,
frequently visited, 1937-41, by Henri
Bergson, great anti-materialist
philosopher. Honoré de Balzac,
1799-1850, supreme Romantic-realist
novelist, born 39 Rue Nationale,
Tours, used many places in Touraine
in novels and short stories, lived at St
Cyr in 1830 at *La Grenadière* (cannot
be visited).

Vieux Tours lies west of Rue
Nationale. Approach it by Rue du
Commerce, the prolongation of Rue
Colbert. At No 25 is the lovely
Renaissance Hôtel Gouin, whose elegant
façade is delicately carved with floral
motifs and coats of arms. Inside is the
Musée de la Société Archéologique de
Touraine whose chief exhibits are of
medieval and Renaissance art, though
archaeology also figures prominently.

Place Plumereau is at the heart of
medieval Tours. All around are brick
and timber gable-ended houses. Most
have been carefully restored following
the damage done during World War II.

Luynes, 8km downstream off the
N152, is an engaging small town on
account of its sixteenth-century houses
and massive fifteenth-century oak
timbered covered market. A walk
through vineyards by the D49 gives a
view of the thirteenth century château.
North of Luynes, a lane climbs for two
kilometres into open farmland on a
plateau. On the right is a long, silent row
of brick supports and six arches which
carried the Roman aqueduct into Tours.

Return to Luynes and continue along
the lane which joins the N152 at Pont-

Traditional interior preserved in Château de Plessis-lès-Tours

de-Bresme. After about three kilometres turn right where a sign says *Monument Historique*. It leads to a conundrum at Cinq-Mars-la-Pile. A huge, forbidding, very ancient, square brick block, 30m tall stands on high ground. There is neither inscription nor decoration. Inside, it is solid. Gallo-Roman, most authorities say. Others argue that it was erected by slave labour (to account for its crude brickwork) when the Alans invaded the region in AD439. No-one knows what La Pile was built for. The château at Cinq-Mars-la-Pile consists

now only of two round eleventh and twelfth century towers whose vaulted chambers can be visited, and from the top are extensive views of the river. The gardens compromise formal French layout with the English liking for naturalness.

Then Langeais, famous for melons and its château. The square keep, put up by Foulques Nerra in the tenth century, may be the oldest extant in France. Louis XI built the royal château between 1465 and 1467, and what you see is as it was six centuries ago. At first glance, a

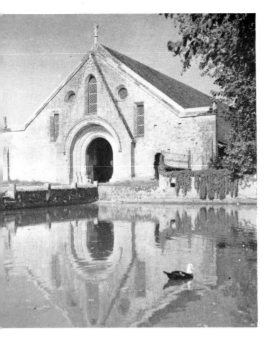

Finest surviving medieval tithe-barn, Grange de Meslay, outside Tours, where Touraine music festival is held

late feudal fortress: parapets, machicolations, round towers, pepper-pot roofs, slit windows, rampart walkways. Interior façades show a Renaissance influence. The fifteenth-and sixteenth-century furnishings form an outstanding collection.

North of Tours the open plateau of the Gâtines Tourangelle offers pleasant runs that are not congested by tourists. The N138 and D959 bring you to Château-la-Vallière where the Etang du Val Joyeux provides camping grounds, a beach and sailing facilties, surrounded by the Forêt du Château-la-Vallière. Another attractive run is from Cinq-Mars-la-Pile by the D34 which passes sizeable lakes before reaching the picturesque ruins of Château de Vaujours (thirteenth and fourteenth centuries), the forest and Château-la-Vallière.

Thirteenth-century Château de Luynes

*La Béchellerie outside
Tours, home of Anatole
France, now a museum*

Every wine lover will seek out
Vouvray, upstream along the N152 from
Tours for about 10km, although there is
nothing very special about the terraced
village itself. Its wines can be tasted and
bought in the viticulturalists' *caves*; a
good Vouvray keeps a long time. Most
of the vineyards hereabouts are quite
small.

Another uncrowded and peaceful run
is along the Cisse valley from Vouvray.
The greatest congestion is at an
enormous duck farm by the roadside.
Take this road at least as far as Nazelles-
Négron, or even further to Pocé-sur-
Cisse and Onzain. Or come back the
same way, turning right at Vernou-sur-
Brenne (its church has a handsome
twelfth-century façade) on the D46
which follows the Brenne valley to the
small industrial town of Château-
Renault where the rivers Brenne and
Gault meet.

*Remaining towers of
medieval castle of Cinq-
Mars-la-Pile*

Aerial view of Château de Villandry and its unique sixteenth-century formal gardens

In marked contrast to the noisy N152, the road west of Tours on the south bank is narrow, quiet, often running along the top of the old *levée* embankment, to provide some of the loveliest views across the Loire. The D88 quits Tours at La Riche and squeezes along the spit that separates Loire from Cher. You can follow it to where the two rivers meet, and double back to Savonnières. This is not to be confused with La Savennières which we visited west of Angers, though both names have the same origin, soapwort, *Saponaria*. The plant, growing plentifully, made Savonnières the laundry depot for the Roman garrison at *Caesarodunum*.

When bruised, the leaves produce a lather to aid the washing process.

Outside the village on the Villandry road are the *Caves Gouttières* or *Grottes Pétrifiantes*, quarries exploited between the twelfth and fourteenth centuries for the Savonnières tufa, easily worked and of a particularly intense white. Countless churches and cathedrals were built with this tufa. Forgotten for 600 years, the *grottes* have calcified into stalactites and other extraordinary concretions. Objects vitrified in the caves can be bought on the spot. The visit lasts about three-quarters of an hour (a glass of wine is included in the charge) and the cave temperature is a steady 14°C, so warm clothing is recommended. During speleological investigations of the connecting galleries, a Gallo-Roman cemetery was discovered, as was a tunnel to the garden of the château at Villandry.

In 2km more you are at Villandry. The château is late Renaissance of 1532. It houses Spanish and Italian paintings: Velasquez, Zurbaran and Goya, Titian and Tintoretto, but the authenticity of some is questionable. Villandry gardens make the place unique. Sixteenth-century designs for a formal French garden have been carefully reproduced. Here it is in three tiers: at the lowest level is the kitchen garden or *jardin potager* where sixteenth-century vegetables and herbs are grown (no potatoes; they had not yet reached France); above that the ornamental garden; uppermost the water-garden and ornamental lake. From this vantage-point are views across Cher and Loire.

For some distance out of Villandry the D16 gives you a very bumpy ride over cobbles, laid down long ago as the *levée* road, and for some reason not resurfaced. For another 20km the prospect of the Loire accompanies you. You pass the tiny fishing centre of La Chapelle-aux-Naux and then

Bréhémont; behind them is fertile, alluvial soil called *varennes*. The rural ride ends at Ile St Martin.

For those who are interested in the application of nuclear energy, the Electricité de France's Centrales Nucléaires d'Avoine-Chinon is 12km further west. You can hardly miss it, for a large silvery sphere is its landmark. There is no charge for going to the viewing platform where models and notices explain the layout and function of the complex installations.

If antiquity makes greater appeal, then go straight from Ile St Martin across the Indre to Ussé on the northern edge of the Forêt de Chinon. Here is a wholly romantic fifteenth-century castle, its white walls and turrets rising out of charming terraced gardens, the whole a backcloth to an operetta, especially when seen from the Loire *levée*. Parts of the interior can be seen over, as well as the isolated chapel in the grounds. Voltaire had a house, *La Henriade*, built at Ussé; 4km in the opposite direction, at Huismes, the surrealist painter Max Ernst lived from 1954 until his death in 1976.

From Ussé, the D7 is the direct route back to Tours (33km).

5 Along the Rivers Cher and Indre

The estuary of the Cher was touched on in the previous chapter when Savonnières and Villandry were dealt with, for the river joins the Loire a little west of Villandry where the railway line between Tours and Saumur has to switch from the left to the right bank of the Loire. The two rivers seem barely able to part company until they begin to drift apart east of Tours, beyond the suburb of St Avertin whose leisure complex uses the Cher. St Avertin owes its name, it seems, to a Scottish monk of the twelfth century who withdrew to the then lonely spot and died there. In June 1940, Château de Cangé at St Avertin saw the meeting between Winston Churchill and the tottering French government, prior to the Franco-German armistice.

Beyond Tours, roads run each side of the Cher, though mostly at some distance from it. The north road, D140, takes you to St Martin-le-Beau which produces a good white wine, but wine connoisseurs will have turned left earlier, setting their sights on Montlouis-sur-Loire. It lies almost opposite Vouvray, though there is no road bridge over the Loire to link the two wine towns anywhere between Amboise and Tours. At Montlouis vines of the Chenin grape cover the south-facing eminence on which the village is built. You can buy wine at the co-operative or, for better quality wines, at private *caves*, many carved out of the chalk. On the quayside, the Renaissance *hôtel*, now a small museum, is the birthplace of the sixteenth-century printer, Christophe Plantin, whose serif typeface is still widely used.

The road along the south bank, N76, goes by St Avertin to Véretz and Azay-sur-Cher. Three kilometres south are some picturesque Romanesque remnants of the Prieuré St Jean-du-Grais. Château de Leugny is a kilometre out of Azay by a drive from the main road. Leugny overlooks the river, and the chief interest is the Louis XVI furniture.

Next comes the township of Bléré with 4,000 inhabitants, facing Ste Croix-en-Touraine on the other side of the Cher. Once known as *Briotreis*, Bléré was a parish founded by St Brice who succeeded St Martin as bishop of Tours. The church of St Christophe was built at different times, the nave being the oldest, perhaps of the tenth century. In the Place de la République is a domed funerary chapel (1526), Gothic in style but Italian Renaissance in its elegant detail.

And so through meadowlands to the village of Chenonceaux whose château, spelled without the 'x', sits astride the Cher. Few will dispute its title of queen of all Loire châteaux. It is not only the beauty, grace, harmony of the architecture and the river setting that leaves an enduring impression. Privately owned and run with imaginative efficiency, the entrance fee gives enjoyable value. A guide is not obligatory; leaflets in English are available; notices explain the furnishings in the apartments; a tea-room and snack bar sells Chenonceau wines; a children's nursery; a little electric train to take you from the entrance along the tree-lined

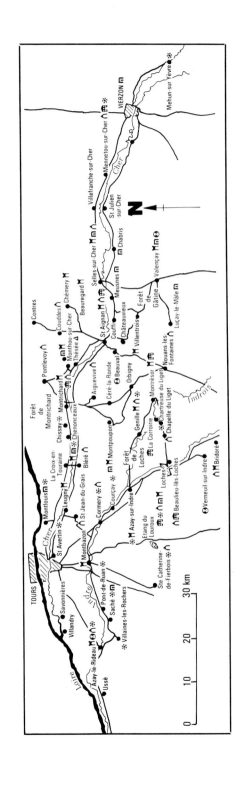

drive if you are so minded; a gift shop; a small waxwork museum of the major figures in the history of the château. And there is *son-et-lumière*. And boat trips along the Cher when the level of the river allows. In short, you can happily make a day of it at Chenonceau.

'*Aux Temps des Dames de Chenonceau*' is the title of the *son-et-lumière* show in the gardens, to emphasise the role of women in the château's history. Built between 1513 and 1521 by Thomas Bohier, chamberlain to four kings, he acquired the property — then a modest working mill — by underhand means for next to nothing. Bohier was sent on a mission to Milan by François I. There he died in 1524. His widow, Catherine Briçonnet, continued supervising improvements, but she died two years later, heavily in debt. The king stepped in, discharged the debts and acquired Chenonceau. When Henri II inherited it, he gave it to his msitress, Diane de Poitiers who spent nine years in

completing the formal gardens, *le Jardin de Diane de Poitiers* today. On Henri II's death, the château went to his widow, Catherine de Medici, who had always loved it. In consolation for being turned out, Diane was given — very generously, it would seem — Château de Chaumont instead. Catherine spent what time she could at Chenonceau with her daughter-in-law, Mary Stuart, making many additions to the building, furnishings, library and park.

The next owner was Louise de Lorraine, wife of Henri III, and daughter-in-law of Catherine de Medici. After her husband had been assassinated, Louise retreated into Chenonceau and for eleven years wore the white robes of mourning, a wraith-like figure spoken of as *La Dame Blanche*.

When the Bourbon court gave up using the royal châteaux of the Loire and moved to Versailles, Chenonceau entered a period of neglect. It was

Montrichard on the Cher, and ruined tenth-century keep

bought by Claude Dupin in 1730. Again, a woman's influence was crucial to Chenonceau's fortunes. After Dupin's death, his wife held intellectual court there: Voltaire, Buffon the naturalist, Montesquieu the political philosopher, were some of the great men of the day to stay there. Jean-Jacques Rousseau was engaged as tutor to Madame Dupin's child in 1746-7. Rousseau was to write later that he enjoyed his period at Chenonceau more than anywhere else in his life. Madame Dupin survived the Revolution, as did her château, through the loyal protection of the people in the vicinity. She lived to be 93.

Her descendants sold Chenonceau in 1864, and another woman dedicated herself to its restoration. The work of conservation has been continued by the present owner, Madame Menier. '*Au Temps des Dames de Chenonceau*' is as apt a title today as it was four hundred years ago.

Montrichard is 8km to the east by the N76 along the north bank of the Cher where the railway line comes between river and road. On the way is the Distillerie Fraise d'Or, 62 Route de Tours, at Chissay-en-Touraine, where you can buy this unusual local strawberry liqueur. The village also had a good looking château which is not open to the public.

On the south bank, the lesser road leads straight to the bridge across the Cher to provide an attractive view of old Montrichard clustering round church and keep. Good hotels, restaurants and recreational facilities make Montrichard (population 3,800) worth staying at. In the ruined square keep started by Foulques Nerra in the tenth century, Richard Coeur-de-Lion was locked up for a while in the tiny cell at its foot. From the top, the town's roofs and church jumble below eye-level; beyond is the river and the distant countryside. A

SHORT EXCURSIONS FROM MONTRICHARD

North of the Cher
Forêt de Montrichard — D764 — Pontlevoy (abbey buildings; road transport museum in cloisters) — D85 — Monthou-sur-Cher — Château du Gué-Péan (sixteenth century, visited by four kings, statesmen, writers; small Resistance museum, as owner was in *maquis*; furnished rooms; pictures from Fragonard to Salvador Dali) — D21 — N76 left — Mazelles — remains of Roman staging-post, *mansio* of *Tasciaca*, on left of road before Thésée — Montrichard.
Total distance 32km.

South of the Cher
D764 — left to ruins of Abbaye d'Aigue-Vive (once famous place of pilgrimage on 8 September for sufferers from St Vitus's Dance (chorea) — Céré-la-Ronde — D81 — pretty run to Orbigny — lanes to west rejoin D764 — right — Château de Montpoupon (feudal castle; collections of old weapons, carriages, hunting trophies, nineteenth-century clothes) — Montrichard.
Total distance 50km.

---

number of fine old houses from between the twelfth and sixteenth centuries survive, as well as some troglodyte dwellings round about the keep. The twelfth-century church saw the pathetic wedding ceremony between 14-year-old Louis d'Orléans and Louis XI's 12-year-old daughter Jeanne-de-France, hunchbacked, crippled and facially deformed, who became a woman of noble character in the face of the adversities which arose in consequence

Photogenic Château de St Aignan-sur-Cher

of her physical afflictions. Just outside Montrichard is Nanteuil church (twelfth and thirteenth centuries) whose corbels of the nave vaults are handsomely carved with human faces; the two-storeyed Lady Chapel was built by Louis XI.

St Aignan is another pretty village of Touraine on the south bank of the Cher. Its château rises impressively on a hill and is most photogenically seen from across the river. Old streets wind up to the château reached by a great sweep of steps. Only the terrace of the château can be visited. From it the view is admirable. Down the hill where there are beam-and-plaster houses, is the early Gothic church whose crypt has frescoes from the twelfth to fifteenth centuries; one of the oldest is most impressive, a Christ in Majesty.

Short excursions round St Aignan can include the Parc Ornithologique de Beauval, 4km south on D675, where endangered species of birds are bred; you can spend plenty of time bird-watching on the estate. To the north of St Aignan is the graceful Manoir de Beauregard (by the D675 to St Roman-sur-Cher and right), skirting the Forêt de Gros-Bois. Chémery, 3km away, has a Renaissance manor house, while the church at Couddes on the D675 has some twelfth-century frescoes on the north side of the nave, and early fourteenth-century ones (Christ in Majesty, Last Judgement, Resurrection) on the south side.

To reach the château at Valençay from St Aignan, two country routes suggest themselves. The longer way borrows narrower roads and goes through Châteauvieux and Villentrois (ruined castle) and the Forêt de Gâtine. Or else, by the D17, turn right after Couffi through Lye to link up at Villentrois.

Valençay consists of two towns *lumière* are weekend features in summer. the *département* of Indre, part of the old province of Berry, always considered to be the true heart of France. The château itself was built by an ostentatious financier in 1540, and successive financiers owned it. The notorious Scot, John Law, 'the father of inflation', would have bought it but for the collapse of the flimsy banking system he introduced into France with the approval of the Regent of France, the Duc d'Orléans. Then, in 1803, Talleyrand acquired the property. Talleyrand (1754-1838), Abbot of St Denis; Bishop of Autun; Prince of the Empire under Napoleon whom he plotted to remove in favour of Murat; head of a provisional government shortly before Napoleon abdicated; intriguer *par excellence* under the Restoration — the great political survivor. a 'very eminent knave', 'that cursèd cripple' said two of his numerous enemies. Talleyrand entertained in high style at Valençay which consists of two ornamental wings at right angles to one another. The west wing is furnished in Empire style, and includes the 'Congress of Vienna' table and mementoes of Prince Talleyrand. A Talleyrand museum is lodged in an outbuilding. The formal gardens contain various animals and birds which roam freely; llamas and flamingoes are the most striking denizens. Some sixty vintage cars from 1898 on, all in working order, can be seen in the Musée de l'Automobile du Centre in the château grounds. *Son-et-Lumière* are weekend features in

Château de Valençay has two museums in its grounds

summer.

In this corner of our region are three flintlock museums, clearly connected to the fact that flint occurs in chalk formations and alluvial soils. Here there is ample high quality silex for the purpose. The first, Musée de la Pierre à Fusil is at Luçay-le-Mâle (Village Retraite, Route de Gehée), 10km south-west of Valençay on D960. How silex is extracted, worked and sold is the essence of the display.

The second museum of the same name is in the *Mairie* at Meusnes, between St Aignan and Selles-sur-Cher, on the D17. Here, too, the story of flint knapping is illustrated. For 300 years muskets were fired by means of flints, and the industry reached its apogee in the eighteenth century. To supply the army's needs 500 knappers were kept fully employed to supply the fifty million flints used annually after the Napoleonic wars, as well as for export to Africa and Latin America. Professional knapping died out in France with World War I.

Yet another such museum, Musée d'Histoire et Traditions Locales, is housed in the cloisters of the one-time abbey at Selles-sur-Cher. In addition to outlining the history of flint knapping, the exhibition reveals the past of Selles, and the implements used by the local *vignerons* of yesteryear.

Selles (from the Latin *cella* or cell, on account of a sixth-century hermit, St Eusice, who lived here) has two châteaux. One is a grim, moated medieval ruin; the other a Renaissance building whose furnished apartments can be visited. The church that venerates St Eusice was built between the twelfth and fifteenth centuries and restored later, and the upper frieze in the apse depicts scenes of the saint's life.

For some distance, the river Cher has been skirting the southern margin of the Sologne with its lakes and forests, an area which will be the subject of a separate chapter. Here, the itinerary stays close to the river. From Selles eastwards, you can again choose between a north and south road. The N76 along the north bank goes through Villefranche-sur-Cher and Mennetou-sur-Cher to Vierzon. The lesser southern route makes for Chabris, St Julien-sur-Cher, St Georges-de-la-Prée into Vierzon.

Mennetou-sur-Cher is an engaging medieval *bourg*, still partly surrounded by ramparts which were erected in 1212. Town gates set in square towers pierce them. La Porte d'En-Bas is the one Joan of Arc passed through on her way to Chinon to meet the Dauphin. Some lovely old houses, the earliest from the thirteenth century, make a walk along Grande-Rue worth while. Part of the church is contemporary with the early houses.

Vierzon, 17km on the N76 from Mennetou, is not a place which attracts many visitors. It is an industrial town making porcelain, glassware and agricultural machinery, and a population approaching 35,000, yet agreeably sited at the confluence of the rivers Cher and Yèvre.

Still on the N76 and 16km south-east of Vierzon, Mehun-sur-Yèvre is an appealing small riverside town. All that is left of the fourteenth-century château is two towers, but we know how the whole looked because of the painting of it by Pol de Limbourg in the *Très Riches Heures* at Chantilly. Mehun's tiny museum displays items saved from the château.

The river Cher, now flowing due south, leaves our region; its source rises at 726m near the hamlet of Cher in Auvergne.

The second valley to be explored is that of the Indre. It creeps into the Loire almost furtively where three islands stand in line in the Loire just west of Néman on D7. As with the estuary of the Cher, that of the Indre is already familiar. In the previous chapter we met it at Ile St Martin and Ussé on D7 which makes its way into Tours. Turn right on to D17. You arrive at another château which has contributed to the fame of the Loire Valley: Azay-le-Rideau.

For beauty it bears comparison with Chenonceau. Of all châteaux, Balzac liked Azay best. Its name is said to derive from a *seigneur*, Rideau or Ridel d'Azay. It could as well have been handed down as a reference to the curtain wall or *rideau* of the castle which stood here previously. Once it was called Azay-le-Brûlé, Azay-the-Burned, when the earlier fortress, held by the Burgundians, was burned to the ground on the order of Charles, aged fifteen — he who was to become Joan's 'gentle Dauphin' — and the prisoners killed.

Screened by tress, Azay, like Chenonceau, is a building of grace and elegance, its white stone edifice well-nigh floating on the river. In fact, it is partly built on piles sunk into the Indre's bed. Azay was created — need one say? — by a financier, Gilles Berthelot of Tours, in the service of the king. It took eleven years to construct between 1518 and 1529. He fell foul of the king and was forced to flee, and François I confiscated the château. A string of owners, forgotten by history, occupied Azay until the French state bought it in 1905. Inside, the building is arranged as a Renaissance museum with period furnishings, tapestries and paintings, as well as its kitchens. There is *son-et-lumière* in summer; the grounds by the river can be visited by a separate entrance if you do not want to see over the château.

Azay-le-Rideau is a charming village. Parts of the parish church of St Symphorien survive from the eleventh century. The local wine is delicate and very palatable.

Before following the Indre, take the southerly road (D57) to Villaines-les-Rochers where an osier co-operative was started in 1849. Today, eighty families, many of them living in troglodyte houses in the village, contribute their extraordinarily varied wicker-work to the modern co-operative building. You can wander round the spacious display hall and observe that the objects for sale are useful as well as decorative. Special varieties of *Salix* osier shrubs are cultivated in the valleys of the Indre and Villaines. *La vannerie* is a traditional craft, handed down over the centuries within certain families. In his *Lys dans la Vallée* Balzac refers to the basket-weavers of Villaines-les-Rochers.

Make your way back to the Indre at Saché. What you are likely to be confronted with before all else in this delightful village is a large, incongruous abstract work in the square. The American artist Alexander Calder (1898-1976) lived at Saché for part of his life and gave this object — a long metal arm on a pedestal balancing at each end a painted disc — to the village. The square is large enough not to be completely overpowered by the stabile. What is called the Château de Saché is a simple sixteenth to seventeenth century *gentilhommière* or manor house of no great merit in itself, and is visited because of the Balzac museum it contains. Between 1829 and 1837 Balzac worked here a great deal through the generous hospitality of friends who owned it. It was his favourite retreat, and Saché strongly influenced his writing. Now, the Balzac museum is a literary shrine, for Balzac is to France what Dickens is to England, and Dostoevsky to Russia. Rooms have been left more or less as they were in his time. There are manuscrips and corrected

Manor house at Saché, famous for its Balzac museum

proofs so minutely annotated in his own hand that the compositors would not work on them for more than two hours a day; anything more brought on eye-strain and headaches. There are figurines of the characters in his *Comédie Humaine*, that enormous portrait of a whole society in ferment and abandoning itself to greed and vice, by a writer who powerfully and prolifically breathed life into the phantoms of his literary creation.

Four kilometres north-east of Saché, the road still following the Indre, is Pont-de-Ruan, where watermills and weirs exhale an atmosphere of riverside indolence on a hot summer's day.

From Pont-de-Ruan onwards, the D17 gets more congested as you approach Montbazon. The town may be famous for a Foulques Nerra fortress, but it has been made ludicrous and vulgar by a nineteenth-century bronze statue of the Virgin on top of what remains of the keep. You are aware of the proximity of Tours, of the N10 (the Poitiers road), and of the *Aquitaine* autoroute. Fortunately, traffic congestion is concentrated, and I would choose to stay at a hotel outside Montbazon for an exploration of the region. Le Moulin Fleuri is a converted mill by the Indre which chuckles past through the grounds of the hotel. Bedrooms are simple and tastefully decorated. The place is run with style, an oasis of quiet off the D87, and is not expensive. No doubt, the famous châteaux-hotels of Montbazon are equally well insulated from the noise of traffic.

Congestion begins to evaporate as you come to Veigné, and the D17 follows the Indre as it bends away from the Loire into a southerly course. Cormery is the first place of historical interest along this road. It is one of the many fortified villages to have been repeatedly pillaged and ransacked by English and French soldiery. Cormery sits pleasantly on the south bank of the Indre, adorned by an old mill and weeping willows. On the opposite bank is Truyes with a Romanesque church whose belfry is in five stages. Although almost nothing remains of Cormery's abbey it is evocative of an older and more pacific Anglo-French association. Founded in 791, the Benedictine abbey flourished for exactly 1,000 years, when the Revolutionary government sold it off for it to be largely destroyed. At the abbey had lived and taught Albinus, better known as Alcuin who had been a pupil at the Cloister School in York. Brought to Cormery in 796 by Charlemagne after having taught the Emperor's children and family at Aix-la-Chapelle, Alcuin of York spent eight years spreading his love of learning. He died at Cormery in 804. His civilising influence was exerted long after his death.

What is left of the abbey is to be found in Rue de l'Abbaye next to the *Mairie* on the N143. The massive eleventh-century belfry-tower arches over the road; the brickwork is in a lozenge and scallop formation, with Romanesque bas-reliefs. A priory lodge and spiral staircase, and arches of the thirteenth-century

EXCURSIONS FROM MONTBAZON

Tours (9km); Villandry (23km); Savonnières (23km); Azay-le-Rideau (22km); Villaines-les-Rochers (21km); Saché (15km); Etang du Louroux (20km); St Jean-du-Grais (old priory) (12km); Chenonceaux (32km); Ste Catherine-de-Fierbois (off N10 after 18km: statue of Joan of Arc in square, *Maison du Dauphin* (1515), church (1498), campanile and statuary).

refectory are other remnants. Also in Cormery is the church of Notre Dame-du-Fougeray (twelfth century) with a single nave and a central cupola. Four twelfth century statues stand in apsidal niches; a cylindrical baptismal font decorated with masks is of the same period; the frescoes are a century later. In the cemetery facing the church is yet another twelfth century religious building, a *Lanterne des Morts*, rare in this part of France but commoner in northern Aquitaine. In the Lantern of the Dead were placed the body awaiting burial, while higher up the tower a lamp would be lit in a small window.

As the D17 potters along beside the Indre the next village is Courçay where you can walk a little way upstream, past cave openings, to a spring. Eight kilometres further on is pretty Azay-sur-Indre whose Manoir de la Folaine (not open) once belonged to the Marquis de la Fayette, much honoured by Americans for his active support in their War of Independence.

That a town the size of Loches (7,000 inhabitants) should have some historical association with the English Plantagenet kings one comes almost to take for granted. There may be a somewhat arcane association for the Scots. Some

Porte Royale

Thirteenth to fifteenth centuries, with Musée Lansyer containing work by local artist and his friends — Delacroix, Doré, Harpignies, Rousseau; Musée du Terroir with reconstruction of Touraine house in nineteenth century.

Château

Tour Agnès Sorel (thirteenth century) with tomb of Agnès Sorel. Logis Royaux, Vieux Logis with tapestries, paintings, mementoes of Joan of Arc and Charles VII; keep (157 steps to top); Tour Ronde; martelet (prison cells); some fortifications built by Henry II.

Eglise St Ours

Unique vaults — octagonal stone pyramids of twelfth century, called *dubas*.

Portes des Cordeliers and Picoys

Hôtel de Ville

(1535-43), Renaissance, has been used always only as town hall; library has manuscripts and record of birth at Loches of romantic poet Alfred de Vigny in 1797.

Renaissance houses in Grande Rue (pedestrians only), Rue des Moulins, Rue St Antoine (Tour St Antoine, sixteenth-century belfry), Rue du Château.

Three shady malls: Mails de la Poterie, Droulin, Donjon.

Beaulieu-lès-Loches

Foulques Nerra buried in ruined abbey; abbey church; Eglise St Laurent; old streets; leper house; thirteenth-century Knights Templars' house; old doorways.

language experts say Loches was once *Luca*, an Indo-European word from which *loch* derives, for Loches was once a Celtic township in the middle of mere and marshes.

Loches contains a whole medieval city, redolent of Ligerian history. Stay a day or two in one of the hotels and sightsee on foot. It also commends itself as a base from which to roam the farm country round about (cattle, goats, pigs, cereals and the so-called 'Paris' mushrooms grown in caves in the vicinity). Loches has a water-sports centre with one heated, covered swimming pool and an open-air one, and tennis courts. In mid-July they hold a Peasant Market. You can ride and

walk along the many tracks in Loches Forest. Cycling and fishing are other outdoor activities. If you are staying between 1 July and 15 September medieval Loches is floodlit at night. By day, you can hire an English-speaking guide.

Loches was a royal château. Charles VII installed his mistress, Agnès Sorel in it. Not that there is anything remarkable about a French king taking a mistress, save that Charles VII did so openly, scandalising public opinion and risking the displeasure of the Church. Agnès has always been singled out for special comment, for she is said to have been the kindliest, gentlest and loveliest of any royal mistress. Pope Pius II wrote of her

lovely face. The recumbent stone tomb in the château suggests these qualities as well as an innocense in her character. What makes her the more interesting is that she was painted by her friend and servant Jean Fouqet (1420-80) of Tours, probably the greatest of any native Ligerian painters. In what is known as the Melun Diptych (hanging in Antwerp) Fouquet paints her as the Holy Mother in his *Virgin and Child* of 1450, the year of Agnès's youthful death.

Montrésor, a village and château of great charm

Perrusson
4km south on N143: church, parts from tenth and eleventh centuries.

Verneuil-sur-Indre
5.5km south on N143, right at St Jean-St Germain, right at next crossroads; gardens of château occupied by horticultural college, open June-October.

Bridoré
14km south on N143, right; château (fourteenth to fifteenth centuries); church of St Roch (fifteenth century).

Forêt de Loches
Largely planted by Vauban to supply ships' timber; four eighteenth-century pyramids, meeting points for hunts.

Chapelle du Liget
8km east on D760, right down lane, right along woodland track; isolated, circular Romanesque chapel built by Henry II, twelfth-century frescoes, domed vaults.

Chartreuse du Liget
0.5km further along D760 from Chapelle du Liget; founded by Henry II to expiate guilt over murder of Becket; dismantled in eighteenth century; impressive eighteenth-century gateway and other buildings (privately owned).

La Corroirie
1km east of Chartreuse on D760, on left in valley at bend in road; annexe of Chartreuse, fortified in fifteenth century (view only from road).

Valley of Indrois
D760 east to Montrésor (9.5km), as beautiful as name suggests, a film-set village, château (part eleventh century), church. 8km east, Nouans-les-Fontaines, thirteenth-century church; fine *Descent from the Cross* in wood by Jean Fouquet (fifteenth century). From Montrésor follow D10 which keeps to sinuous Indrois valley, tree-lined meadows, fruit trees, vines, to Genillé (10.5km), fifteenth century château, sixteenth-century church, cave dwellings. St Quentin-sur-Indrois (7km), delightful setting. Azay-sur-Indre (7km) — Loches (10km).

The bodice round her slim waist is unlaced to expose one breast (she enjoyed showing her breasts at court); her head is shaved and crowned; the face is long, pinched, expressionless, yet she is a woman of real flesh. Not at all a Virgin of medieval piety, but a wordly figure belonging to Renaissance scepticism.

We know from the same source what her lover, Charles VII looked like.

Fouquet painted him about five years after Angès's death. As one critic has put it, the 'head is subtly but coldly described: timid, melancholy, secretive, self-doubting', much as history remembers that pathetic king.

South-east from Loches the Indre goes deeper into Berry where it becomes the Dark Valley of the works of George Sand, and to its source in the low hills of Limousin.

Chaumont

Chambord

Bourges Cathédral

6 From Amboise to Blois____

It is time to return to the main artery, the Loire, at Amboise. With a population of 11,500 its narrow streets magnify the bustle of a small town into that of a mini-metropolis. Pedestrian shopping precincts and car-park facilities are the compensations. Some shops in the precincts sell such local delicacies as *rillettes* (potted pork), goat's cheese and *pâtisseries*. A number of hotels and restaurants are concentrated on Quais Charles Guinot and Généal de Gaulle; both overlook the Loire.

The visitor is offered liberal distractions: *son-et-lumière*, '*Soirée à la Cour du Roy*' at the château in July and August is a spectacle of local dancers, riders, jugglers. There are concerts; wine fairs in April and August; Sunday morning markets; wine *caves*. In high summer, guided tours of the town are available. Outdoor activities include cycling, walking, riding, tennis, swimming (open air and covered pools), fishing, water-sports. There are camping sites on the Ile d'Or and outside Amboise; holiday camps; youth hostels; various types of letting accommodation.

Beginning as a township of wooden houses and palisades founded by the Carnutes, it attracted the eye of Caesar's lieutenant Crassus who made it his winter quarters and named it *Ambacia* after the little tributary La Masse which flows into the Loire to the south. It is said that the Roman walls were still standing in 1646 where now is Place St Denis. The caves below the plateau on which the château stands have been called 'Caesar's granaries', and wheat may well have been stored in them.

Amboise, as was mentioned in 'History in Brief', was the meeting place of Clovis, king of the Franks and Alaric II, king of the Visigoths, in 503. When the Arabs reached the outskirts of Tours in the eighth century, they may have got as far as Lussault-sur-Loire, 6km west of Amboise on N751 because two localities there are known as '*Camp des Arabes*' and '*La Caverne des Sarrazins*', but such seemingly straightforward associations need to be taken with two grains of salt.

During Viking invasions, the people of Amboise were massacred at Négron, but history centres itself chiefly on the château where two earlier medieval castles had stood. A third had been in the town lower down. Charles VIII and his wife Anne of Brittany (thus Brittany became a province of France) began rebuilding the château in 1492. He was clearly a young man of taste, vision and impatience. Workmen had to labour day and night whatever the weather. Two years later he campaigned in Italy. Dazzled by the richness of its art, Charles transferred to Amboise booty, artists, craftsmen, scientists and gardeners of Renaissance Italy, 'this terrestrial paradise', he exclaimed. At Amboise he had the formal garden laid out in Italian style. What is visible now of the château is only a fragment (but a fine one) of the original. Before his premature death in 1498, Charles bought the manor house of Le Clos-Lucé, a little to the south-west of the château.

The next king, François I arrived at Amboise at the age of six to complete an

Manor house of Clos-Lucé, Amboise, home of Leonardo da Vinci for the last years of his life

all-round education. The first three years of his reign were spent here creating a brilliant, diverse and stimulating life at court. His love of the arts led him to try and persuade Michelangelo to come to France, but without success. Leonardo da Vinci (1452-1519) did come from Italy in 1516. François gave him a pension and the use of Le Clos-Lucé (then called Cloux) until his death. Andrea del Sarto (1486-1531), the most important painter in Florence, came to Amboise in 1518-19, but broke his contract with the king to return to his wife.

Leonardo, the universal genius of the Renaissance, spent the last four years of his life at Le Clos-Lucé, an honoured guest. His intellectual powers anticipated later discoveries in aeronautics, engineering, anatomy; he invented the armoured car, the submarine, aircraft and the helicopter, though they were not actually constructed. In those last years, he probably did not paint, perhaps on account of a crippling paralysis, but there is a sketch of Amboise in Windsor Castle. Much of Leonardo's time was taken up with designing costumes for *fêtes* and pursuing scientific ideas, including a scheme for draining the Sologne by means of a canal between Romorantin and the Loire.

The visual arts in France were to be dominated by the High Renaissance which had been transported from Italy to Amboise. As François I built new palaces nearer to Paris this influence spread. Fontainebleau was the most important medieval building to be transformed by the Renaissance cult

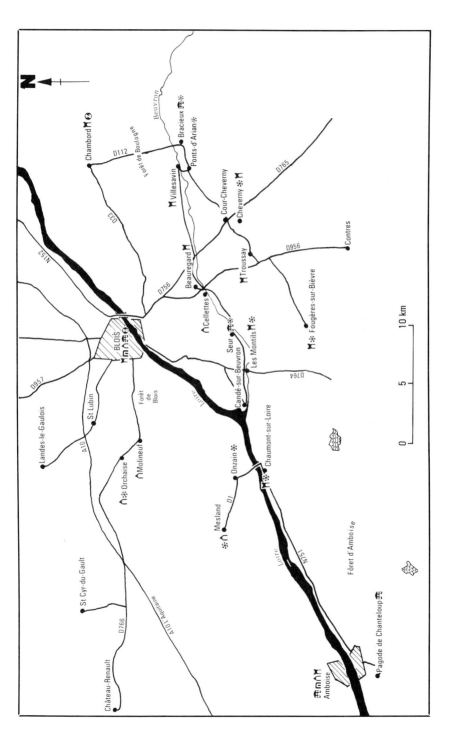

99

Château

Best seen from Tours road (N152).
Entrance between sixteenth-century
Hôtel de Ville (historical documents,
Aubusson tapestries) and Church of
St Florentin (once Notre Dame-de-
Grève or Strand, marking flood-tide
levels).
Plaque to Joan of Arc (23-24 April,
1429).
Terrace over Loire; garden; bust of
Leonardo.
Fifteenth-century Tour d'Horloge.
Tour Hurtault.
Flamboyant Chapelle St Hubert
(1491) on battlement, said to contain
bones of Leonardo (under stone of
chapel floor); modern stained glass
windows.
Logis du Roi (Gothic and
Renaissance wings); furnishings;
tapestries.
Tour des Minimes or Tour des
Cavaliers (with ramp for
provisioning château).

Manor-House of Le Clos-Lucé

Leonardo da Vinci museum; garden.

Old streets and buildings round foot
of château: Rue Léonard Perrault
and Porte des Lions (François I had
menagerie of lions and other wild
animals in dry moat of château);
Porte de l'Horloge; 6 Rue Joyeuse
with Musée de la Poste, models of
coaches, uniforms, engravings, start
of letter-post in seventeenth-century
France.

*Château d'Amboise, Salle des Etats where
Protestants were sentenced after 1560
uprising*

uprising of Protestants led to their
massacre at the château in the presence
of Mary Stuart, Mary Queen of Scots,
wife of François II. When, a century
later, the château fell into the hands of
the rebellious Gaston d'Orléans, the
king, Louis XIII, felt obliged to have the
defences demolished. More was pulled
down after the French Revolution when
it became a prison. The nation acquired
Amboise château in 1975.

On leaving the château, swing left
along Rue Victor Hugo with its
attractive old houses. At the end is Le
Clos-Lucé to which Leonardo travelled
over the Alps on mule-back, carrying
some of his paintings including two of
the most celebrated pictures in the
world, the *Mona Lisa*, painted some
twelve or more years earlier, and *The
Virgin of the Rocks*. Clos-Lucé is a
charming little pink brick and white

both architecturally and pictorially.

The story of Amboise moves on to the
sickening Conjuration (or Tumult) of
Amboise when in 1560 a misconceived

stone building. The rooms are carefully and appropriately furnished, but interest focuses on the four rooms which make up the Leonardo museum. Models have been made from his plans by IBM engineers, an astonishing variety of realisable ideas thought up centuries before they were actually made to work. The north courtyard is laid out as a Renaissance garden. Beyond is a small park which slopes towards the La Masse stream.

South of Amboise is the lake-studded Forêt d'Amboise where Valois kings once hunted. If you take the D61 southeast you come to Bois de la Moutonnerie where there are signposted walks. The D31 out of Amboise brings you in 2.5km to a right turn to the Pagoda of Chanteloup. It is a folly, all that remains of Château de Chanteloup, built by the Duc de Choiseul in 1771. He had been Chief Minister to Louis XV but was banished to his château for having

displeased Madame du Barry. Here he entertained in the grand manner, did some farming (of which Arthur Young had no high opinion), and hunted. A later Duc de Choiseul, Jean-Antoine Chaptal, chemist and minister under Napoleon, immortalised his own name in *chaptalisation*, the process (sometimes abused) by which sugar is added to wine to strengthen it. The château was pulled down in the last century.

Look again at the 44m high folly beside a pool. If you are reminded of the pagoda at Kew you would be right; the duke had copied it. You can climb to the top and see the forest stretched out below.

Take the quieter south bank road (N751) upstream from Amboise to Chaumont-sur-Loire, for its lovely river views and wine villages where Gamay reds can be tasted and bought.

The château at Chaumont sits in handsome confidence on the highest

Pagoda of Chanteloup, an imitation of the one in Kew Gardens

spur of rock of any along the banks of the Loire. From the village — just one long street — the climb is quite an effort. High-walled, with massive round white towers and pepperpot roofs, Chaumont was built in the late fifteenth and early sixteenth centuries on the site of much earlier castles. Looking more medieval than Renaissance, the exterior is the most worthwhile part of a visit, not only for its splendid appearance but also for the views from the eighteenth century terrace, for its grounds with ancient cedar trees, and its spacious stables put up in 1877.

Compared with others, the château at Chaumont has had a relatively pacific history. Its chief notoriety is that Catherine de Medici gave it to her late husband's mistress, Diane de Poitiers, in exchange for Chenonceau. Diane did not much relish the arrangement and soon abandoned Chaumont for her château at Anet. The interior of Chaumont was transformed and modernised at crippling expense from 1875 onwards until financial disaster hit the owners. It has been State-owned since 1938. If the interior is less interesting than the outside, there are some tapestries, terracotta medallions, Renaissance furniture, and the rooms of the two rivals, Catherine and Diane, to be seen.

A bridge over the Loire gives you a chance to see something of the opposite bank. Onzain is a sizeable *bourg* beyond the delightful Cisse valley referred to in Chapter 4. It is known for its cheese and wine from the Mesland vineyards, 4km north-west on the D1. Mesland is interesting, apart from its wines. It was known as Fontaine-Mesland until the middle of the eighteenth century because its fountain was thought to possess healing properties. All manner of Gallo-Roman finds testify to the antiquity of the place, and Richard Wade supports

Corner of game reserve at Chambord

the view that Mesland derives from *Hermèslande* (Hermes Heath), Hermes having been a Romanised Gaulish god, the horned *Cernumnus*. The porch of the Romanesque church of 1060 has twenty-six stylised, helemeted and bearded (*barbus*) heads, very reminiscent of Gaulish carvings of head-hunting warriors in the museums of Aix-en-Provence and Marseille. Inside the church are twelfth-century fonts, a Virgin and Child of the thirteenth century, and another of the sixteenth century from the Abbey of Marmoutier.

Northwards beyond Mesland the land rises towards the plateau of the Beauce. You can wander along quiet lanes which link one inconspicuous village with another, some with evocative names such as Landes-le-Gaulois, Champigny-en-Beauce, St Cyr-du-Gault. A dolmen or two, streams, small lakes, relics of once extensive forests, and farmlands whose commercial centre is Blois.

The main road into Blois (D766) comes from Château-Renault and crosses the A10 autoroute. From Orchaise (Carolingian sculpture over the church entrance, picturesque mill, Fontaine d'Orchaise in a grotto) the road passes through 11km of the Forêt de Blois, once a huge oak forest. At Molineuf-sur-la-Cisse, the church of St Secondin dates back to the eleventh century, as does the one at St Lubin-en-Vergonnois on the Cisse north-east of Orchaise.

For the visitor, Blois with 49,500 inhabitants, is one of the major centres along the Loire. It had been the capital of the once powerful Counts of the Blésois region, rivals to the Counts of Anjou. Seen from the south bank it seems to cascade gracefully towards the river from its knoll. Indeed, for the pedestrian, this is an up-and-down town — and worth the effort. Old houses clustering around the château and

---

SOME THINGS TO DO IN BLOIS

Tourist Information Office, 3 Avenue Jean Laigret.

Railway station: frequent services to Paris (178km).

Car hire services, and bicycle hire.

Son-et-lumière, 'Spirits love the Night' at château; also concerts.

Guided visits round Blois. Coach Tours.

Five cinemas.

Tennis courts; two swimming pools; water-sports centre on Loire at Blois-Vineuil with swimming pool, mini-golf, water-skiing, wind-surfing, sailing, boat-hire, pedalos, picnic-areas, camping sites, refreshments.

Forest walks and riding.

Hotels, restaurants, youth hotels.

Light aircraft trips from Blois-le-Breuil.

---

cathedral are being carefully restored after serious destruction in 1940. The upper part of Blois is a pedestrian precinct. Most of Blois lies on the north bank of the Loire and the château is the chief attraction. A splendid royal château until 1589 when Henri III died, emblems of its royal associations are everywhere. The emblem of Louis XII was a porcupine carrying a crown; Anne of Brittany had a cord and ermine tails; François I a crowned salamander spitting fire; the initial L (Louis XII), A (Anne of Brittany, his wife), and F (François I).

A stroll along the picturesque streets of Old Blois rewards you with half-timbered houses and mansions, and you

Château
Guided visits all year to courtyard; Chapelle St Calais; Galerie Charles d'Orléans; Louis XII wing and Musée des Beaux-Arts; François I wing, apartments and outside staircase; audio-visual history of château; small archaeological museum of Gallo-Roman finds at Blois; Salle des Etats-Généraux.

Pavillon Anne de Bretagne
(*Office de Tourisme*), erected by Louis XII (fifteenth century) of stone and brick, attached to half-timbered Orangery (also Louis XII).

Eglise St Vincent
Seventeenth century, north side of Place Victor Hugo.

Jardin du Roi
Above Place Victor Hugo, remains of royal gardens of château.

Musée Robert-Houdin
5 Rue de la Voûte-du-Château, museum devoted to original magician Houdini (1805-71), not American escapologist who later took same name.

Façade des Loges and Façade Gaston d'Orléans
Buildings exterior to château walls.

Maison Hué-Bodin
Rue de la Voûte-du-Château, old established house selling canvas designs for tapestry-making; designs from fifteenth century on.

Eglise St Nicolas
Steps down from Place du Château (twelfth and thirteenth centuries), considered to be most successful blend of Romanesque and Gothic architecture in whole of Loire Valley.

Fontaine Louis XII
Place Louis XII, copy of original (in wretched state) in château.

---

can glimpse into the courtyards of some of them. Start from Place de l'Ave-Maria, east of the château and walk along Rue de la Fontaine-des-Elus; Rue du Puits-Châtel; Rue des Papegaults (No 10, Hôtel Belot, see round courtyard); Rue des Juifs (No 3, Hôtel de Condé, see courtyard); Rue Pierre-de-Blois; Rue St Honoré (Hôtel d'Alluye can be seen over during office hours); Rue Chemonton; Rue du Lion-Ferré.

For a not too concentrated visit to some other famous châteaux of the Blésois a round trip of about 75km can take in Chambord, Cheverny, Beauregard and Fougères.

First, Chambord. From Blois cross the Loire by the eastern bridge and turn left on the D33 which leads straight to Chambord whose château is on the northern edge of the village. This is the largest of all Loire châteaux, the megalomaniac creation of François I, an expression of grandiosity which is the perpetual temptation to absolute rulers. François had it built after his return from Italy in 1519. Innumerable architects and masons added to it. Leonardo may have had a small hand in its design. It was not finished by the time François died in 1557. Previously, a fortified hunting lodge of the Counts of

Escaliers Denis Papin
Steps and statue of Papin (1647-1714), inventor, discoverer (according to French) of principle of steam-engine in 1707 (counterclaimed by British for Marquess of Worcester's steam pump of 1655).

Cathedral of St Louis
Sixteenth century, destroyed by whirlwind, rebuilt in seventeenth century; tenth- and eleventh-century crypt.

Hôtel de Ville
Eighteenth century, former bishops' palace and gardens.

Tour Beauvoir
Rue Beauvoir, twelfth-century keep.

Notre Dame de la Trinité
Rue Monin, completed 1949; 60m high campanile (240 steps); fine carillon of forty-eight bells, concerts in summer; outstanding stained-glass windows.

Pont Gabriel
Bridge across Loire, built in 1717.

Eglise St Saturnin
Fifteenth to seventeenth centuries.

Chapelle Notre Dame-des-Anges
Quai Villebois-Mareuil. Contains pilgrims' *ex-votos*.

Cimetière St Saturnin
Opposite church, cemetery dating from François I, enclosed by four covered, timbered galleries, rare in France; small lapidary museum (same ticket as for château).

Chocolatie Poulain
Avenue Gambetta, tours arranged after telephone appointment on weekdays. (See further information for details).

Blois had stood on the swampy site. This was demolished. In its place had to go a château that was larger than anybody else's. A few statistics give an idea of the vast ambition: 156 metres by 117 metres, flanked by six massive towers; 440 rooms; 14 main staircases; 70 secondary ones; 800 capitals; 365 chimneys. Teams of hundred upon hundreds of workmen were drafted to build the cheerless folly. The façade is an enormous film-set extravaganza; the interior impresses by its extraordinary staircases, the forest of sculpted chimneys. A walkway round the château offers a panorama of the surrounding park, itself enclosed by the longest wall in France, 32km in extent. François I was a passionate hunter; Chambord was his fantastical hunting-lodge where he entertained lavishly. Leonardo even designed the first 'mobile homes' to accommodate the overflow from the château. But the place was uncomfortable and never properly lived in. Various kings paid brief visits; Molière performed two plays there in the presence of Louis XIV. Louis XV was the last royal resident. Every owner wanted to be rid of it; the State bought it in 1930.

You visit Chambord to see a few state rooms, the amazing spiral and double-

Floodlit Cheverny whose exterior is exactly as when built in the seventeenth century

ramped staircase, the cross-shaped, vaulted *Salles des Gardes*, the chapel, the apartments of Louis XIV and François I, and the terraces. On the Michelin map a large part of the park is shown as a *Réserve Nationale de Chasse*, so pedestrians are allowed only into the western part of some 1,200 acres, plus four observation posts in the *Réserve* from which you can watch deer and boars feed, but permission has to be granted.

Chambord was where the idea of *son-et-lumière* was born, during a dramatic thunderstorm, a most appropriate place at which to stage historical drama.

South from Chambord, the D112 slices through the Parc de Chambord and Forêt de Boulogne to Bracieux (8km). Bracieux lies on the fringe of the Sologne and is a pleasant old town on the banks of the Beuvron crossed by a charming bridge. A sixteenth-century covered market is surmounted by a tithe-barn.

Three kilometres west and following the Beuvron is Ponts d'Arian (Hadrian's Bridges), for the village lies on the Roman road which came from Chartres. Cross the river to reach the small and modest Château de Villesavin, built in 1537 by François I's financial secretary who was in charge of paying for the building of Chambord. Erected by Italian workers employed on Chambord, Villesavin is very much an Italian Renaissance creation down to the Carrara marble used in it. The kitchens are of interest, and there is a display of horse-drawn vehicles and some rather dilapidated frescoes. Note the pigeon-loft, complete with its revolving ladder. The loft was for 1,500 pigeons: a precise figure because of the legal nicety that an owner was allowed one pigeon to every acre in his possession; any more would

2,000 pairs of antlers in the hunting museum at Cheverny

annoy the neighbours.

Return to Ponts d'Arian and turn right on to the D102 for Cour-Cheverny. On the far side of the *bourg* is another celebrated château, Cheverny. Its harmonious unity of style was achieved because the dignified white tufa-stone building was put up to an unaltered plan in thirty years, between 1604 and 1634. Nor has it ever been altered or its façade cleaned on account of the tufa whitening with age. You are shown the

handsomely proportioned and furnished rooms; the King's Room is the most striking; the *Grand Salon* has paintings by Titian, Mignard and of the School of Raphael.

Outside, the pack of hounds in their kennels can be seen, as can the Hunting Museum, of interest to anyone who enjoys looking at 2,000 pairs of antlers. This is hallowed hunting country. In winter meets are held twice a week when the huge, ornate coiled horns, the

A somnolent, delightful stream to be followed by minor roads as far as Bracieux where it enters the Sologne, subject of a later chapter. Candé-sur-Beuvron where the stream enters the Loire — D7 to Les Montils (remains of twelfth-century fortress; basket-weaving workshop) — D77 to Seur (old public wash-house) — watermills — Cellettes (thirteenth- and fourteenth-century church with reliquary of St Mondry, sixth century hermit invoked as protector of vines) — Ponts d'Arian — Bracieux.

Trompes de Cheverny, pierce the air with their high-pitched slightly cracked sound. As the extensive grounds are not open to the public, you can do no more than glimpse the handsome trees through the railings.

Four kilometres west is the small Renaissance *gentilhommière* of Troussay, restored in the nineteenth century. The owner brought to the château various items such as sculptures, windows or flagstones from various monuments in the district which have now disappeared. Outbuildings by the courtyard house collections of old agricultural implements and domestic utensils of yesteryear.

Continue west from Troussay until you strike the D956 going north. Beyond Cellettes, on the right, is the next place of call on this châteaux-crawl from Blois — Beauregard. This modest and elegant building had been the home of Jean de Thiers, minister under Henri II, and friend of Ronsard. The visit is made more interesting by virtue of the gallery of 363 portraits of people well known in the late sixteenth century.

From Château de Beauregard to Blois is seven kilometres through the Forêt de Russy.

Fougères-sur-Bièvre has not been included in this circuit; there will have been more than enough châteaux for one day. To reach Fougères, follow the D956 from Blois for 14km, turning right at the D52 crossroads for another 7km. The little château is in the centre of the town, itself an agreeable place to walk round. In contrast to the other Blésois châteaux, Fougères is something of a throwback to feudal times. Defence rather than show-off exposure was uppermost in the minds of the builders. Begun in 1470, when other Châteaux had already abandoned purely military considerations, Fougères was erected with the English invasions and the reconquest of the lands by Joan of Arc's armies still in the memory. Later generations of owners were to soften its grim appearance.

7 From Blois to Gien

From Blois the Loire sweeps in a semi-circle northwards, with Orléans at its zenith. To the south is Sologne to be visited in the next chapter. The N152, still following the river along its north bank, is now the most interesting road in spite of the traffic. A château of great elegance is Ménars, 7km out of Blois. Its central part was built in 1637. Madame de Pompadour acquired it in 1760 and had two wings and four pavilions added; her brother laid out the terraced gardens at the bottom of which are the carved heads of Pompadour and her rival Madame du Barry. At the time of writing the château is closed.

At Suèvres (where old houses go down to the Loire) turn left for the sixteenth-century château of Talcy (15km) on the Beauce plain. Externally severe, within it has the feel of a bourgeois household of 400 years ago. Its charm and interest is enhanced by the association of three poets with it. Ronsard stayed at the château and wrote love poems to the fifteen-year-old Cassandra, daughter of the owner. Agrippa d'Aubigné fell in love with the same owner's grand-daughter, dedicating his verses to her. Great-grandson of Cassandra was the

Château de Ménars and statue of Emperor Augustus

109

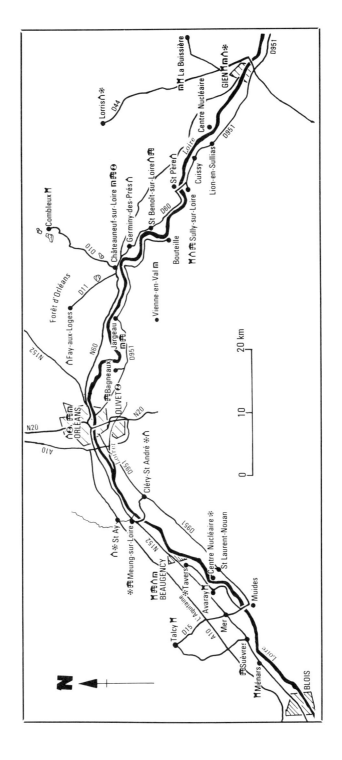

romantic poet Alfred de Musset. Talcy's greatest claim to historical fame is that in 1562 Catherine de Medici arranged a meeting of Protestant and Catholic leaders in her unavailing effort at reconciling their bitter differences.

The D15 leads back to the N152 at Mer. If you want to see the *Centre Nucléaire*, the nuclear power station, take the Loire bridge south of Mer, turn left at Muides on D951 to St Laurent-Nouan. Left again and at the *Centre* the observation platform overlooks the complex; models and diagrams explain the working of the station.

A more distant prospect of the *Centre Nucléaire* can be gained from the north bank by turning off N152 at Mer and taking the little riverside road to Avaray (Louis XIII château). It goes on to Tavers, old, watered by resurgent streams and fountains; its vanished castle for long belonged to the English crown. Beaugency is a compact little town of 7,300 inhabitants, which looks very attractive from across the river, and might tempt the visitor to stay a few days. It was captured on four different occasions by the English during the Hundred Years' War before Joan of Arc relieved it.

Meung-sur-Loire is also Meung-sur-Mauve because the stream, coming down off the Beauce divides briefly into three at Meung before rejoining to flow into the Loire. Once they drove the many mills (a few are still working) that ground the cereals grown on the Beauce plateau. One watermill, Le Grand Moulin, is an art gallery. Along the Quai du Mail is the stone statue of Jehan de Meung (1240-1305), native of this town. It was he who added 18,000 more stanzas to the already celebrated poem, *Le Roman de la Rose*, written fifty years earlier by Guillaume de Lorris. To the romantic and allegorical love verses of the original, Jehan added a penetrating

---

WHAT TO SEE IN BEAUGENCY

Eglise Notre Dame
Twelfth century, badly restored; fine organ; modern stained-glass windows.

Place Dunois
In front of church, lit at night by antique lanterns.
Tour du Diable
Part of the medieval fortifications. Donjon (keep), known as Tour de César, eleventh century.

Tower of St Firmin
Church destroyed during Revolution.

Château Dunois
Fifteenth century, with *Musée des Arts et Traditions de l'Orléanais* (regional ethnology museum).

Hôtel de Ville
Renaissance, restored; contains tapestries and embroideries.

Grand and Petit Mail
Mall shaded by trees, with views of valley.

---

satire on the philosophical conventions of his day, criticising both royalty and the church. He revealed himself as a Renaissance humanist in the Middle Ages; his influence on later writers was profound, for his verse was a prototype of character analysis dear to French writers.

Another poet, François Villon, was held captive in the Château de Meung from 1459 for two years and tortured before his release under the king's amnesty. In going round the well-furnished château you see the *oubliettes* where Villon languished. Rabelais also

Talcy, a château with poetical associations

Beaugency, eleventh-century Donjon de César and twelfth-century church of Notre Dame

Beaugency, Renaissance Hôtel de Ville

see also his private chapel, and the one used by his more amiable cousin, the Bastard of Orléans, who continued Joan's work of clearing the English out of France after her death. He, too, was buried here. Under a slab to the right of the nave is where the heart of Louis XI's son was placed. Huguenots destroyed the original oak statue of the Virgin and put up a replica in the sixteenth century. In the richly decorated Chapelle St Jacques are examples of the apparel and utensils carried by medieval pilgrims. The stalls and south door were donated by Henri II; they bear his royal initials and, brazening convention, those of his mistress, Diane de Poitiers. The names of important visitors to the basilica since 1325 are carved in the nave.

For its size (105,000 inhabitants, nearer a quarter of a million with its outlying parts) Orléans, it is fair to say, offers relatively little of major importance to the sightseer. Hotels, restaurants, shops and city distractions there are in plenty. Perhaps it is too big for instant affection. Reconstruction work after widespread wartime destruction has been carefully done; the area round the cathedral was least touched by bombing.

Understandably, Orléans — a royal city *par excellence* — makes the most of its brief, dramatic association with Joan of Arc. Every 7 and 8 May the Joan of Arc Festival is held with a panache of fervour and fireworks to honour the Maid who had herself, in 1430, instituted this thanksgiving for deliverance.

To the south, on the tongue of land between Loire and Loiret, is Faubourg St Marceau whose numerous horticultural establishments provide the flowers you see everywhere in Orléans. Its roses, in particular, are famous. Roses, as well as other plants, are grown in the *Jardin Botanique* in Quai de Prague. A rural atmosphere emanates from the tree-

knew Meung, staying at the Grand Cour at St Ay, 6km along the N152; the fountain is known as Fontaine Rabelais. The church of St Pilhard (eleventh to thirteenth centuries) is cruciform, rare among Loire Valley churches.

Across the river is an ancient place of pilgrimage, Cléry-St André; it is still observed on 8 September and the following Sunday. In 1280, peasants found in a bush an oak statue of the Virgin. A small church was erected. The miraculous find drew huge numbers of pilgrims already on this route towards Compostela in Spain, and proved highly profitable locally until in 1428 during the Hundred Years' War the Earl of Salisbury ordered the demolition of the church; only its square tower remains. A rather stark Gothic basilica replaced it, chiefly at the instigation of Louis XI who often stayed in the house (now a school) to the right of the church. He and his wife were buried at Cléry. His statue is an 1894 reproduction. You can

Place du Martroi
Equestrian statue (1855); high reliefs on plinth depict episodes in her life.

Cathedral
In the chancel Joan gave thanks for first victory over English; chapel dedicated to Joan, and statue of Cardinal Touchet (instrumental in having her canonised in 1920) kneeling before St Joan (1914); nineteenth-century stained glass windows showing her life.

Musée Historique et Archéologique
Hôtel Cabu, Place Abbé Desnoyers. Fifteenth-century German tapestries, seventeenth-century banner used in Joan of Arc festivals.

Maison Jeanne d'Arc
Place du Général de Gaulle. Reconstruction of house she stayed at in 1429; audio-visual account of entry into Orléans on 8 May 1429; contemporary costumes, arms, models.

Quai Fort-des-Tourelles
Plaque and cross commemorating fifteenth-century fort held by English in 1428 prior to relief by French forces; statue of Joan (1804).

Centre Jeanne d'Arc
24 Rue Jeanne d'Arc. Documents on St Joan in Orléans.

Hôtel de Ville
Statue of Joan at foot of steps — copy of original marble in Versailles by Marie d'Orléans, daughter of King Louis-Philippe.

Rue de Bourgogne
Street of triumphal entry.

Eglise St Paul
Reconstructed since 1945; chapel of Notre Dame des Miracles where Joan gave thanks for deliverance of Orléans.

---

shaded, narrow road along the north bank of the Loiret where you can see a couple of watermills, small pleasure craft, graceful swans and fishermen.

South of the Loiret is Olivet, virtually a suburban extension of Orléans. Here are more nurseries and the *Parc Floral de la Source*, delightfully planted out with flowers in seasonal succession, trees and lawns. A miniature railway, a little zoo and a restaurant make the *Parc* a popular attraction. Opposite the *Parc Floral* are the new university buildings laid out in the American style.

The Loiret is a curious river. It emerges, fully grown, as it were, from a pool occupied by flamingoes and other birds in the *Parc Floral* to flow 13km into the Loire. Its actual source is at Bouteille, 26km away near St Benoît-sur-Loire, where it starts as a subterranean tributary of the Loire's bed before emerging in rhythmical pulsations from its pool at Olivet.

Twenty-five kilometres out of Orléans is Châteauneuf-sur-Loire (6,000 inhabitants), an attractive place to stay a few days. Grievously bombed in 1940, it has been faithfully rebuilt. There are shady walks along riverside paths, a bathing beach and swimming pool, a covered market-place and street arcade. The park of the château is famous for its rhododendrons and azaleas (the 'English Garden'); the 'French Garden' is in front of a very large orangery, and the

Orléans, annual Joan of Arc festival in front of cathedral

650. To enhance its prestige, the abbot arranged for the remains of St Benoît and his sister, St Scholastica, to be stolen from the ruined abbey of Monte Cassino in southern Italy. A 'strip-cartoon' in stone on the lintel of the north door of the basilica tells this story. The church of Ste Scholastica is in the next village.

Pilgrims and wealthy patrons came as the abbot had hoped. St Benoît became a centre of learning, medicine, the arts and agriculture. Monks built roads and bridges, drained and farmed. So wealthy did the order become that, in order to transfer money safely from one place to another, it invented letters of credit. Louis VII borrowed money from the Benedictines to finance his disastrous Second Crusade of 1147. With the Revolution the abbey was declared national property, its wealth appropriated, and the Benedictines were

moat is filled with carp. But the chief interest is the *Musée de la Marine de Loire* in the château's rotunda. It tells the history of the Loire boatmen and the craft they used; models, tackle, clothes, documents, photographs bring vividly to life the commercial exploitation of the river in the past.

St Benoît-sur-Loire is 10km from Châteauneuf. Its basilica of St Benoît (St Benedict) has been a major centre of Christian hagiolatry, and of religious importance long before. This whole fertile region had been regarded by the Gauls as being at the centre, physically and spiritually, of their territories. Each year Druids gathered in conclave. When the followers of St Benedict came they found the people to be pagans in need of conversion. A monastery was founded in

Statue of Joan of Arc in Orléans

115

Cathedral of Ste Croix
Rebuilt between 1601 and 1829; nine
chapels of thirteenth century; vestiges
of fourth-century sanctuary and
tenth-century church in crypt;
treasury.

Rue Royale
Arcades and shops; in 1791 William
Wordsworth lodged in it, falling in
love with Annette Villon; their
daughter Caroline was christened in
the cathedral.

Rue de Bourgogne
Shops.

Nouvelles Halles
Covered market for food.

Salle des Thèses
Rue de Bourgogne. Remnant of old
university library (apply at Préfecture
opposite).

Eglise St Aignan
Rue Coligny. Fifteenth century;
apply 2, Impasse St Aignan.

Musée des Beaux-Arts
Hôtel des Créneaux (sixteenth
century), Place de la République.
Outstanding collections of paintings
of Siennese and French Schools,
pastels, busts, portraits, modern

artists including Max Jacob who
lived at St Benoît-sur-Loire.

Musée Historique et Archéologique
Rue Ste Catherine. Prehistory,
superb Gallo-Roman items from
Neuvy-en-Sullias (33km east of
Orléans) — bronzes found in 1861,
part of temple treasure: horse, stag,
boar, bull, running man, tightrope
walker, dancer, *danseuse*, all dated to
the first century AD; ivories.

Centre-Musée Charles Péguy
Maison d'Euverte Hatte
(Renaissance, restored), 11 Rue du
Tabour, Museum of Péguy (1873-
1914, born in Orléans) with
memorabilia of poet, writer,
polemicist who espoused many
conflicting political and religious
causes with great integrity; killed
early in World War I.

Old Town
Mansions (mostly restored): Hôtel
Groslot, Place de l'Etape; public
garden and façades of Pavillons
d'Escures (early seventeenth
century); Hôtel Toutin, Rue Notre
Dame de Recouvrance (sixteenth
century).

Musée des Sciences Naturelles
Rue Marcel Proust. Aquaria,
dioramas of animals.

unable to return until 1944. The present
church was built in 1218 and, although
much restored, is a fine example of
Romanesque architecture, and the
Gregorian chant sung during services is
a widely admired musical experience.

Both towers were taller in the Middle

Ages than they are now. Most striking
aspects are the belfry porch-tower, nave,
transept and chancel (note the Italian
mosaic of the tenth century on the
floor). St Benedict's remains are in the
eleventh-century crypt.

'*Le Port*' says the signpost (and the

Forêt d'Orléans

Largest French state forest, mainly oak and Scots pine; mammalian and avian wild life; pathways (some marked); ponds round Combleux (sixteenth- to seventeenth-century château); disused Canal d'Orléans; Etang de la Vallée (water sports); Orléans Golf Club; Fay-aux-Loges (eleventh- to thirteenth-century church).

Bagneaux

Farmhouse off D951, last home of Isabelle Romée, Joan of Arc's mother.

Vienne-en-Val

Museum, Route de Tigy, second century Gallo-Roman sanctuary; sculptures of Jupiter, Vulcan, Mars, Venus, found under church square in 1968.

Jargeau

Joan of Arc statue in Place du Martroi; old town gates; restored medieval riverside houses; Musée Oscar Roty, 3 Place de Petit-Cloître, with modern sculptures and engravings, and house arranged as nineteenth-century peasant dwelling; traditional *Foire aux Chats* (Chestnut Fair) every mid-October.

Germiny-des-Prés

(Germiny-of-the-Meadows). Lovely little Carolingian church of 806 in early Romanesque style of cruciform plan with four apses; nave added in fifteenth century; magnificent ninth-century mosaics in cupola of east apse (uncovered in nineteenth century) of 130,000 coloured glass pieces on theme of Ark of Covenant, taken from Ravenna; early fonts; alabaster windows; wooden statue of Ste Anne and infant Virgin; other treasures in vestry; Lantern of the Dead outside; row of tamarisks in garden — a pink screen in May.

Between Bouteille and Jargeau: river embankment (*levée*) drive.

Michelin map). Some old houses testify to a once active commercial river traffic by the quiet reach.

Sully-sur-Loire, 18km upstream on the left bank, was two-thirds demolished in 1940 and 1944 but has been carefully restored and is an engaging small town. Only the château, the church of St Ythier and the tall spire of St Germain church escaped serious damage.

The château commands the passage of the Loire. Neat, clean and well restored since 1962 when it was bought by the *département*, its image shimmers in the broad moat fed by the Sange stream. Its strong round towers and pepperpot roofs make it a fourteenth-century fortress outside. Inside, although scantily furnished, the size an decorations of the apartments and their chimneys allow the visitor to visualise them as comfortably lived-in rooms. Most remarkable is the upper part of the keep whose medieval timbers are wonderfully preserved — among the best in France.

There are three salient historical associations with the château: Joan of Arc was held prisoner in 1430; Duc de Sully, Chief Minister to Henri IV,

Château
Rebuilt 1484, damaged in 1940, restored, with *Musée International de la Chasse à Tir et de la Fauconnerie* (Hunting and falconry museum).

Eglise Ste Jeanne-d'Arc
1950-4.

Faïencerie
Pottery works on the D952, western extension of Quai Lenoir, guided visits by arrangement; *Musée et Salle d'Exposition*, guided visits arranged at office in Place de la Victoire.

Excursions
Lorris (26km), ancient royal town, church, forest. Château de la Bussière (12km), moat, lake, fishing museum and aquarium, exhibition of ancient vehicles. D951 southwards follows river and canal to Sancerre and northern Auvergne.

Carvings in thirteenth-century basilica of St Benôt-sur Loire

Château de Gien, part of the international hunting museum

planted out the park; Voltaire in exile wrote and performed his plays here. Concerts and plays are given each summer as part of the Sully Festival.

Across the suspension bridge (which collapsed in January 1985 as a result of the severe winter weather) is St Père-sur-Loire whose church of brick and wood is post-war.

Follow the attractive but narrow *levée* road through Cuissy to Lion-en-Sullias. On the other side of the Loire is a new Electricité de France nuclear power station. In another 13km you reach Gien, our last town on the Loire. From the south bank its handsome riverside buildings, tree-lined *quais*, and the château rising above them are placed in perspective by the arched bridge.

8 The Sologne and Bourges

The Sologne is flat. An imaginative response to it is to sense sadness and isolation, a dour self-sufficiency and polite silences. The dark and crouching domestic architecture seems to hark back to past poverty and inhospitality. The more prosaic eye sees varied forest, broken by heaths and meres, threaded by deserted country lanes, the sunlit broom of early summer and rich autumn colours of trees and heather, the birdlife round the pools.

However you see it, the Sologne differs geologically from the neighbouring lands. It is a soft, marshy region of poor soils which many generations have struggled to reclaim. It is neither a historical province nor a modern *département*; 'the land without a name', Alain-Fournier called it in his famous fantasy-novel, *Le Grand Meaulnes* (1913). It is a *petit pays* (though well over a million acres in extent) which nobody much wanted when the *départements* were created. In 1790 the bulk of the Sologne was given

La chasse, a major preoccupation in the Sologne

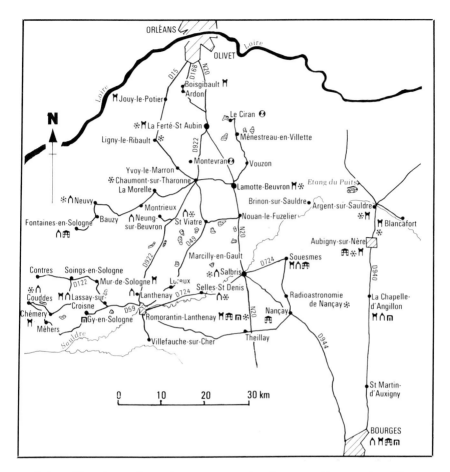

to Loir-et-Cher; the northern piece went to Loiret; the eastern remainder to Cher.

Its ancient forests were for long almost impenetrable. Even the upheavals of the Hundred Years' War and the Revolution of 1789 scarcely penetrated this archaic and impoverished countryside, better cultivated under the Romans than in the early nineteenth century. In the eleventh century some meres, or *étangs*, formed part of a drainage system under the auspices of monks from surrounding monasteries: Marmoutier, Pontlevoy, Fleury (St Benoît-sur-Loire), Selles-sur-Cher, St Aignan, and by the Counts of Blois and the Dukes of Orléans. The region then was self-supporting. Then came neglect, rural exodus and endemic malaria. Not until a century ago did substantial improvements begin: creation of credit, reafforestation, large-scale agricultural co-operation and the introduction of new techniques and crops, drainage, marketing. More recently, new roads have opened up the Sologne to tourism, and an old and distinctive way of life and language has all but vanished.

Architectural traditions more or less mark out the limits of ethnic Sologne. Houses and farms were once low buildings of wood and cob (clay, gravel and straw); they gave way to equally low timber-framed and dark red herringbone brick dwellings which are still common and identify the region. They make a rough circle a little south of the great loop in the Loire, follow part of the Cher, turning north where the Sauldre enters the Cher. Chambord and Cheverny — dealt with in an earlier chapter — both encroach slightly on Solognot territory.

Few districts elsewhere in the Loire Valley can offer a more profoundly rural holiday. Certainly, there are small châteaux, museums, churches (many with narrow, pointed spires of dark grey slate, on small square towers), small towns, villages and tourist attractions, but it is the natural environment which is the source of pleasure. For the walker, tempting-looking paths may lead only to jealously guarded private properties. Get permission to enter, or stick to the signposted tracks of the two *Grandes Randonnées* which meander across the Sologne: GR31 from Sancerre to Bracieux, and GR3c from Gien to La Ferté-St Cyr where it links up with GR31.

The main motoring artery through the Sologne is the N20 south from Orléans through Olivet, La Ferté-St Aubin, Lamotte-Beuvron, Salbris and Vierzon. The projected A71 will run nearly parallel to the N20. Within the triangle bounded by the N20 between La Ferté-St Aubin and Salbris, the D922 (La Ferté-St Aubin to Romorantin-Lanthenay, the chief tourist road), and the D724 (Romorantin-Lanthenay to Salbris) is the main concentration of small, shallow lakes. They are the outstanding feature. Some are reed-lined, others overgrown. A few are covered with water-lilies (*nénuphars* in French). There are hundreds of pools, but no two are totally alike. The bird-watcher comes into his own provided he does not trespass. Make friends with a large-scale farmer, landowner or game-keeper first; you may then be given access to off-the-beaten-track pools where the bird life is rich and undisturbed. I pick a few names at random: harriers, waders, gulls, terns, warblers, geese, cranes, herons, bitterns, ducks. In autumn the watcher will spot regular arrivals of waders, geese, raptors and cranes. One of the sensory delights is to be startled by the sudden sound of a splashdown of a flight of water birds, and then the silence returns, or when the quiet air is split by the derisive laughs of ducks.

Agreeable hotels can be found in or just outside some of the small towns: St Martin-d'Auxigny, Brinon-sur-Sauldre, Chaumont-sur-Tharonne, Romorantin-Lanthenay, Nouan-le-Fuzelier, Nançay, Ouchamps are examples (there are over twenty *Logis de France*) of places which make suitable centres from which to get to know the Sologne.

I will pick Chaumont-sur-Tharonne arbitrarily. It is a pleasant village of under 1,000 inhabitants, standing on a raised *motte*. Ramparts once surrounded it and moulded the village to its present circular plan. In the village square is a quiet, creeper-covered old hotel, La Croix Blanche whose comfort, service and food are highly praised. It is not cheap to stay here — and why should it be when the all-round excellence is sustained? — but this is a base of charm in the western part of the Sologne.

Coming to Chaumont from Orléans are two minor roads which are to be preferred to the N20. Both cut across La Sologne Orléanaise. The D15 goes a little to the south-west out of Olivet. It passes Jouy-le-Potier whose Château du Lude is surrounded by a moat fed by the river Cosson. Then Ligny-le-Ribault where, by the roadside, you see in slight amazement a large nineteenth-century brickworks, complete with an old, round

Montevran Zoo
4km north on D922, then left; wild animals in 45 acres of park.

Lamotte-Beuvron
10km east on D35; château (sixteenth to eighteenth centuries) acquired by Napoleon III in 1852 to create a model farm. Only *Mairie* in France to bear Napoleon III's arms. Home of the Demoiselles Tatin, ladies who one day by mistake produced an upside-down apple tart, now a celebrated sweet called *Tarte Tatin*.

St Viâtre
11km south on D123; charming *bourg*. Fifteenth-century church with four sixteenth-century painted panels of lives of Christ and St Viâtre (from *viator*, voyager), sixth-century hermit. Brick built fifteenth-century repository of St Viâtre at north entrance to village, once pilgrimage centre to pray for relief from 'fever of Sologne' (malaria); custom died out after drainage of marshes round village and introduction of quinine after 1850. Village known as *Tremblevif* until 1854.

Fontaines-en-Sologne
West via La Marolle-en-Sologne, Montrieux-en-Sologne, Neuvy (pleasant site; church; old farmhouse), Bauzy — 36km. Twelfth-century church fortified in seventeenth century; note Angevin vaulting in single nave. Good examples of houses in traditional style.

Ménestreau-en-Villette
Domaine Solognot du Ciran (east to Vouzon, left through Ménestreau, left in 3km on D108 — 26km); bird sanctuary.

Neung-sur-Beuvron
13km south-west; midnight mass in church, offering of lamb by shepherds.

---

kiln and every sort of tile, brick and pipe stacked about. After Yvoy-le-Marron is Chaumont.

Or you can take the D168 from the centre of Olivet. Beyond some military installations is the seventeenth-century Château de Boisguibault on the right before Ardon. The road joins the N20 which goes into La Ferté-St Aubin. Round the seventeenth-century château are some traditional Sologne houses of brick and timber and flat-tiled roofs, squat upon the ground. Turn off the N20 and Chaumont is reached in 14km.

A larger centre than Chaumont to stay at is the capital of the Sologne, Romorantin-Lanthenay. Only in recent years has the name become double-barrelled; it is more convenient to refer to it as plain Romorantin. With a population of 18,100, the town has a diversity of industries, and has been prosperous since the fifteenth century, drawing its wealth from clothmaking. In 1810 there were 115 small factories with 2,500 employees. It had been important enough for the Black Prince to lay siege to it in 1356.

It sits astride the river Sauldre. Corners of the *vieux quartier* are both charming and interesting, as are the views from the bridges. Perhaps the best

Old Renaissance Houses
Chancellerie, brick and timber; Hôtel
St Pol, stone, and brick varnished
green and blue; Hôtel de Pierre
(fifteenth century); Le Carroir Doré,
carved wooden corner posts of
Annunciation and St Michael slaying
dragon, Archaeological Museum
within; more old houses on south side
of Sauldre.

Town Hall
Musée Solognot with arts, costumes,
traditions; reconstructed *locature* or
peasant farm interior; reconstructed
workshop of clogmaker (clogs worn
into this century to suit Sologne
clay); municipal library with copy of
original edition of Montaigne's
Essays.

Royal Château
Much restored remains of fifteenth-
century château where future
François I lived.

Chapelle St Roch
In north-east suburb of St Roch;
erected after plague of 1584-5.

Square Ferdinand Buisson
Public gardens overlooking Sauldre.

Eglise St Etienne
Fifteenth century, on islet in Sauldre;
noted Angevin vaulting.

Musée de la Course Automobile
Museum of Racing Cars, 29
Faubourg d'Orléans: museum and
library of Matra racing cars (Matra
factory in east of town).

Lanthenay
Church with painting of Virgin
between John the Baptist and St
Sebastian (sixteenth century)
attributed to Timoteo Viti, mannerist
Umbrian painter; sixteenth-century
wooden statues.

known of any hotel in the Sologne is the
old coaching inn, Grand Hôtel du Lion
d'Or, its reputation based on its cuisine
and general comfort, for both of which
you pay very substantially. Much more
moderate accommodation is to be had in
the town and in the village of
Lanthenay, 2.5km north of Romorantin.

Two short itineraries from
Romorantin let you see something of
southern Sologne. First, the D59 to the
west of the town brings you to one of the
most agreeable of Sologne châteaux.
Château du Moulin is 1.5km outside the
village of Lassay-sur-Croisne. Built of
red and black brick between 1480 and
1502 by Philippe de Moulin, it remains
furnished in the style of his times. See
the vaulted kitchen and huge chimney,
the interior courtyard and its fifteenth-
century well. A painting of the château
as it was before the addition of the east
tower is in the small fifteenth-century
church of St Denis in Lassay; there is
also a fresco of St Christopher done at
the end of the fifteenth century.

North of Lassay is Mur-de-Sologne
whose sixteenth-century moated
Château de la Morinière stands buried in
woodlands. Take the Contres road as far
as Soings-en-Sologne (Roman urns
found here are in the museum at Blois,
and a Roman statuette is displayed in
Tours), turn left and just before
Rougeou, turn right. You come to
Chémery whose Renaissance manor

Clogs once the universal footwear in marshy Sologne

to Méhers, Billy and Gy-en-Sologne where there is a museum of old agricultural implements, the *Locature de la Straize*. The return to Romorantin by D59 is a pretty route past some lakes.

From Romorantin, the main road (D724) to Salbris first goes to Selles-St Denis. The church of St Genoulph (twelfth to fifteenth centuries), or St Genou (St Knee), owes its curious name to a saint venerated locally and nowhere else. It was believed that he had the power to cure rheumatism and ailments in the legs, and in the fifteenth century the church attracted many pilgrims. In the church are sixteenth century frescoes which depict thirty-four scenes from the saint's life and miracles. Rue de l'Englise contains Solognot houses of timber and brick.

Salbris (its Celtic name was *Saldobrivoe*, 'bridge over the Sauldre') was an important Roman station at the crossroads of the Orléans to Bourges and Blois to Bourges highways. Its church of St Georges (twelfth to sixteenth centuries) has a *pièta* from the Abbaye St Sulpice in Bourges. Steam

house is near the Etang de l'Arche. Chémery's more prosaic claim to fame is that natural gas, piped all the way from Lacq in south-west France, is stored here and then distributed to Paris.

A fairly narrow road west takes you past the sizeable Etang de Bonneuil to Couddes whose church has twelfth-century frescoes on the north wall of the nave, and fourteenth-century ones on the south wall; the theme of the former is St Christopher appearing before King Dannus, and the latter shows Christ in Majesty, angels of the Last Judgement and the Resurrection of the Dead. From Couddes, a gentle run along lanes leads

Radio-telescope at Nançay as it was in 1962, then the largest in the world

railway enthusiasts should enquire at the *Syndicat d'Initiative* about local excursions.

Souesmes, 11km east of Salbris, was another important Roman station at the crossroads of the Orléans to Bourges and Auxerre to Tours roads. Roman antiquities are housed in the archaeological museum at Romorantin (which also contains pottery and many other objects found in an important dig of 1885 at Montrieux-en-Sologne). In addition to tenth-century remnants in its church, there are old houses and mills in and outside Souesmes (some are on the Pierrefitte-sur-Sauldre road). The Château de Souesmes (fourteenth to sixteenth centuries) on its *motte* has a central tower which serves as a staircase.

Due south for 9km on the D29 is the Radio-astronomy Observatory of Nançay, possessing one of the largest radio-telescopes in the world. There are explanatory notices and tapes, and guided visits take place on the second Saturday of each month at 2.30pm by previous written arrangement. Nançay village contains artisans' studios whose collective works are exhibited at the Grenier de Villâtre.

From Nançay back to Romorantin is 32km. With the exception of Theillay on which seven roads converge, you will not pass anything larger than a hamlet.

To see something of the heartland of the Sologne leave Romorantin by Faubourg St Roch along the D49 for Loreux, through the Forêt de Bruadan (another name of Celtic origin) to Marcilly-en-Goult, St Viâtre and Nouan-le-Fuzelier on N20. This route allows you to meander among the densest concentration of lakes. Nouan has two good hotels, both in the Sologne countryside away from the main road. Either makes an admirable centre from which to visit the more easterly margin of the Sologne.

A town that should not be missed — least of all by the Scots — is Aubigny-sur-Nère. *'La Cité des Stuarts'* announce the signs on the approach roads. In 1189 Aubigny (*Albiniacum* in Roman times) became part of the royal domain and prospered. Charles VII enlisted Scottish help against the English, and in 1423 gave Aubigny to John Stuart of Darnley, his Constable, in recognition of his services to the French king. A succession of distinguished Stuarts reigned at Aubigny until 1672 when the last male heir died. Although it reverted to Louis XIV he gave it to Louise de Keroualle, Duchess of Portsmouth and mistress of England's Charles II. Aubigny was held by her descendants — the Dukes of Richmond — until 1834. Scottish artisans were brought over and industries such as glassmaking and cloth weaving flourished for 200 years. Until

Immense interior of cathedral of St Etienne, Bourges

the nineteenth century, the town was known as Aubigny-les-Cardeux or Carders. Numerous streets with early sixteenth-century houses survive. Their oak beams came from the Forêt d'Ivoy in which the Stuarts had their summer residence, the Château de la Verrerie — the Glassworks Château — itself as delightful as is its lakeside setting, 10km from Aubigny along the D89. It was given to the Stuarts by Charles VII in addition to the town.

In Aubigny, the town hall was once the château of the Stuarts. Next door are the graceful public gardens, *Le Parc de la Duchesse de Portsmouth*. The Stuart arms are to be seen on the town hall, the *Maison du Bailli* and the church of St Martin. Down by the river, three round towers are all that remain of the original ramparts.

North of Aubigny on D940 is another pleasant little town, Argent-sur-Sauldre. Its château gardens are open to the public. East of it is Blancafort, yet another picturesque place. By the river Grand Sauldre is the pink brick fifteenth-century château and its grounds. The apartments are furnished. West of Argent by D948 and D765 is the handsome, tree-lined Etang du Puits, spaciously laid out for water-sports enthusiasts.

Southwards from Argent-sur-Sauldre, D940 makes its Roman origins apparent by travelling straight as an arrow back through Aubigny-sur-Nère and La Chapelle-d'Angillon. At the latter, the Château de Béthune was the birthplace of Alain-Fournier and included in the

Cathedral of St Etienne

Begun in 1185, finished 1323, later additions and restorations. One of the largest Gothic cathedrals in France; immense interior; five asymmetrical west-face doors with sixty-two bas-reliefs; majestic nave supported by huge columns and grouped colonettes; thirteenth-century stained-glass windows are among finest in France; largest crypt in France, marble figures; ascent of north tower, views over Bourges. Audio-visual show, *'Trésors d'Art du Cher'*.

Jardin de l'Archevêché

Next to cathedral.

Palais Jacques Coeur

Rue Jacques Coeur. One of the most splendid examples of Gothic domestic architecture; fifteenth-century mansion built for Charles VII's Master of the Mint, Jacques Coeur.

Hôtel Cujas

4 Rue des Arènes. Sixteenth-century mansion; includes *Musée du Berry* with Italian, French and Flemish paintings; folklore; exhibition of old domestic furniture; archaeology.

Hôtel Lallemant

6 Rue Bourbonnoux. Fine cloth-merchant's Renaissance mansion; contains museum of decorative arts.

Museum d'Histoire Naturelle

Rue Messire Jacques.

Jardin des Prés Fichaux

Overlooking river Yèvre.

Hôtel des Echevins

Rue Edouard Branly. Fifteenth-century town hall; decorated octagonal tower, circular stairs.

Guided tours of medieval quarters and cobbled streets from Office de Tourisme, 14 Place E. Dolet.

---

conducted tour is a video-recording about him. In the church of St Jacques are inscribed the names of soldiers who lost their lives in 1914; Alain-Fournier's is among them; his parents are buried in the adjoining cemetery.

The road then slices through the oak and beech Forêt de St Palais to Bourges. Physically, if not historically, removed from the Loire Valley, Bourges (66km from Romorantin and 76km from Chaumont-sur-Tharonne) makes a stimulating contrast to the unassuming quiet of the Sologne, either as a day's excursion or to stay at. With a population of 79,400, most of the things a visitor will want to see are confined to the old, central part of Bourges.

Château of La Verrerie

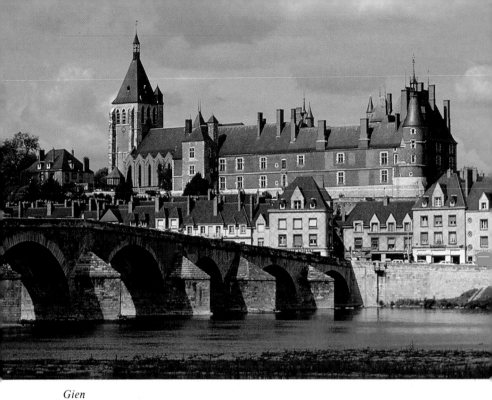

Gien

Ninth-century mosaic, Gérminy-des-Prés

Further Information

INFORMATION AND BOOKING CENTRES

All major tourist towns, as well as numerous smaller places, have a tourist information centre called *Office de Tourisme* or *Syndicat d'Initiative*. At the smaller resorts, these offices are likely to be open only during the summer season. They provide free information about hotels, camp sites, local amenities, excursions, special events, museums, châteaux and *son-et-lumière* events, and wine-tasting addresses. Local guide books may also be on sale (or else ask at the nearest bookshop).

Associated with the *Office de Tourisme* in larger towns is the *Accueil de France* which makes same-day (and not more than five days in advance) hotel bookings. These facilities are available at:

Angers (Maine-et-Loire)
Place Kennedy
Tel: (41)88 69 93,
and Place Gare St Laud
Tel: (41)87 72 50

Blois (Loir-et-Cher)
Pavillon Anne de Bretagne, 3 Avenue Jean Laigret
Tel: (54)74 06 49

Orléans (Loiret)
Place Albert I
Tel: (38)53 05 95

Tours (Indre-et-Loire)
Place Maréchal Leclerc
Tel: (47)05 58 08

Separate from the above are officially backed booking offices which make reservations at hotels, self-catering accommodation (*gîtes*) which are sited mostly in rural areas and villages, at camp and caravan sites. In addition, special activity and sports holidays can be booked. Centres where bookings of this nature can be made (the service is usually free) and where a member of staff speaks English are:

Maison du Tourisme, Place Kennedy, BP 852, 49008 Angers
Tel: (41)88 23 85
for hotels and self-catering accommodation (*gîtes*) in Maine-et-Loire *département*.

Loisirs-Accueil, 11 Place du Château, 41000 Blois
Tel: (54)78 55 50 or 78 47 43
for car and camping car hire, sail-boarding, canoeing, barge-journeys, horse-drawn caravans in Loir-et-Cher *département*.

Loisirs-Accueil, 3 Rue de la Batonnerie, 45000 Orléans
Tel: (38)62 04 88
for horse-drawn caravans, houseboats, barges, canoeing, fishing, sail-boarding, craft holidays in Loiret *département*.

Tourist information offices at other important but smaller tourist centres in the Loire Valley are at:

Amboise (Indre-et-Loire)
Office de Tourisme, Quai Général de Gaulle
Tel: (47)57 09 98

Ancenis (Loire-Atlantique)
Office de Tourisme, Place Pont
Tel: (40)83 07 44

Aubigny-sur-Nère (Cher)
Syndicat d'Initiative, Mairie
Tel: (48)58 00 09

Beaugency (Loiret)
Office de Tourisme, 28 Place Martroi
Tel: (38)44 54 42

Bourges (Cher)
Office de Tourisme, 14 Place E. Dolet
Tel: (48)24 75 33
(Bourges is placed in this list because, although it lies on this book's periphery, it is a major centre).

Château-du-Loir (Sarthe)
Syndicat d'Initiative, Mairie
Tel: (43)44 00 38

Château-Gontier (Mayenne)
Syndicat d'Initiative, Mairie
Tel: (43)07 07 10

Châteauneuf-sur-Loire (Loiret)
Office de Tourisme, Place A. Briand
Tel: (38)58 44 79

Chinon (Indre-et-Loire)
Office de Tourisme, Place de Général de Gaulle
Tel: (47)93 17 85

Doué-la-Fontaine (Maine-et-Loire)
Syndicat d'Initiative, Place Hôtel-de-Ville
Tel: (41)59 18 53

La Flèche (Sarthe)
Syndicat d'Initiative, 23 Place Marché-au-Blé
Tel: (43)94 02 53
and Maison de Tourisme, Boulevard Montréal
Tel: (43)94 49 82

Gien (Loiret)
Office de Tourisme, Place Gabriel Péri
Tel: (48)75 20 03

Langeais (Indre-et-Loire)
Syndicat d'Initiative, Mairie Tel: (47)96 71 62

Loches (Indre-et-Loire)
Office de Tourisme, Place Marne
Tel: (47)59 07 98

Le Lude (Sarthe)
Syndicat d'Initiative, Place F. du Nicolay (1 June-15 September), and 8 Rue Boeuf (15 October-31 May, closed Sundays and Mondays)
Tel: (43)94 62 20

Montoire-sur-le-Loir (Loir-et-Cher)
Syndicat d'Initiative, Mairie
Tel: (54)85 00 29

Montreuil-Bellay (Maine-et-Loire)
Syndicat d'Initiative, Place des Ormeaux
Tel: (41)52 32 39

Montrichard (Loir-et-Cher)
Office de Tourisme, Grands Degrés de Ste Croix
Tel: (54)32 05 10
and at Mairie, Tel: (54)32 00 46

Richelieu (Indre-et-Loire)
Syndicat d'Initiative, Grande Rue
Tel: (47)58 13 62

Romorantin-Lanthenay (Loir-et-Cher)
Syndicat d'Initiative, Place Paix
Tel: (54)76 43 89

St Aignan (Loir-et-Cher)
Office de Tourisme (1 July-31 August)
Tel: (54)75 22 85
At other times Tel: (54)75 13 31

Saumur (Maine-et-Loire)
Office de Tourisme, 25 Rue Beaurepaire
Tel: (41)51 03 06

Sully-sur-Loire (Loiret)
Office de Tourisme, Place de Général de Gaulle
Tel: (38)35 32 21

Vendôme (Loir-et-Cher)
Office de Tourisme, Rue Poterie
Tel: (54)77 05 07

Vierzon (Cher)
Office de Tourisme, Place Gabriel Péri
Tel: (48)75 20 03

SON-ET-LUMIERE

Son-et-lumière (the phrase has been incorporated, for all practical purposes, into the English language) was born in the Loire Valley. The first performances were given at the château of Chambord in 1952. *Son-et-lumière* has now spread world-wide. Even after more than thirty years, it still makes a dazzling finale to a holiday in the region. Not to have experienced one such display is to deprive oneself of the dramatic recreation of local history, made more remarkable still on a fine summer's evening as darkness falls. Each château presents the theme of its main historical events. Its erstwhile life is given sumptuous dimensions where actors in period costume re-enact the past.

Scenarios, titles and times of performances may alter. Check times of the next performance locally (particularly as the times given in the list which follows are only a very general indication). Up-to-date information is available at the château itself, at the local tourist office, your hotel, and on street advertisements.

This is not a cheap form of entertainment. Entrance fees are lower for parties than for individuals. Special rates apply for children.

Local coach operators run evening package tours. Again, the local tourist office will have details.

Amboise (Indre-et-Loire)
'*A la Cour du Roy François*', a Renaissance

party at the royal castle. 420 actors in period costume. On certain dates between end of June and mid-August, starting around 10pm (90 mins).

Azay-le-Rideau (Indre-et-Loire)
'Puisque nous n'avons autre visage'. At Easter, and from last weekend in May to last weekend in September, starting around 10pm (60 mins).
Information, Tel: (47)61 61 23

Blois (Loir-et-Cher)
'Les Esprits aiment la nuit' in French and English. On some days in April, and between end of August to end of September; daily at other times in summer (closed Thursdays except in July and August). English version at 10pm or later (30 mins).
Information, Tel: (54)74 06 49

Chambord (Loir-et-Cher)
'Le Combat du jour et de la nuit'. Between late April and end September, starting at 9.30pm or later (35 mins).
Information office: Régie du Spectacle de Chambord, 95 Avenue de Verdun, 41000 Blois
Tel: (54)78 67 68, or at Chambord, Tel: (54)46 31 32

Chaon (Loir-et-Cher)
'Raboliot, livre vivant', actors in period costume. On certain evenings in July, starting at 10.30pm (120 mins).
Information office: Centre Régional de Culture Populaire, 9 Avenue de Toulouse, Nouan-le-Fuzelier, 41600 Lamotte-Beuvron.
Tel: (54)88 71 09

Chenonceaux (Indre-et-Loire)
'Aux Temps des Dames de Chenonceau'. (Note: it is customary to spell the village with an 'x' and the château without.) At Easter and between mid-June and mid-September, starting at 10pm or later (90 mins).
Information: Château de Chenonceau, Chenonceaux, 37150 Bléré.
Tel: (47)29 90 07 or 29 93 52

Cheverny (Loir-et-Cher)
'Cheverny à la lueur des flambeaux', on a theme of a Renaissance hunting party. Late July to mid-August (60 mins).
Information: Château de Cheverny, Cheverny, 41700 Contres.
Tel: (54)79 96 29

Chinon (Indre-et-Loire)
'Charles VII, l'enfant maudit', actors in period costume. Nightly between mid-June and mid-September at 10pm.
Information, Tel: (47)93 17 85

Fougères-sur-Bièvre (Loir-et-Cher)
Actors in period costume, and pyrotechnics. A few evenings in July at 11pm.
Information: Comité des Fêtes Communales, Mairie, Fougères-sur-Bièvre, 41120 Les Montils.
Tel: (54)46 26 50

Le Lude (Sarthe)
'Les glorieuses et fastueuses soirées au bord du Loir', five centuries of history with 350 actors in period costume, 300 fountains. Between second weekend in June to first weekend in September, starting around 10pm (105 mins). On Friday and Saturday evenings, fireworks display (supplementary charge).
Information, Tel: (43)94 62 20

Valençay (Indre)
'La Reine Margot', actors, musicians and horsemen in Renaissance costume. Weekends between early July to early September (150 mins).
Information during *son-et-lumière* season: Syndicat d'Initiative, 36600 Valençay.
Tel: (54)00 04 42
At other times: Château de Valençay, BP 23, 36600 Valençay
Tel: (54)00 14 33

CHÂTEAUX OPEN TO THE PUBLIC

The châteaux listed here are mostly those which charge an entrance fee to see over them, and in some cases over their gardens as well or separately. A few which can be viewed only from outside the building make no charge. Many more than can be included in this book are not open to the public but can be glimpsed from the roadside in passing.

The words 'open daily' are to be understood as meaning open both morning and afternoon with about a two-hour lunch break. In July and August some places remain open continuously throughout the day. Afternoon closure times vary according to the season. Some châteaux are open on French public holidays; most are closed on at least some of them. Public holidays are: New Year's Day, 1 January; Easter Day and Easter Monday; Labour Day, 1 May; VE Day, 8 May; Ascension Day; Whit Sunday and Whit Monday; Bastille Day, 14 July; Assumption Day; All Saints' Day; Remembrance Day, 11 November; Christmas Day, 25 December. In addition, many châteaux close on one weekday (Tuesday is the commonest). All details of opening days and times should be checked locally, as there can be changes at short notice.

Day and evening (for *son-et-lumière*) coach trips to local châteaux during the season are available at many tourist resorts. Some are accompanied by English-speaking guides. Enquire at local tourist offices.

Châteaux, followed by their nearest towns, are listed by *départements*. If only the name of the château is known, the alphabetical index gives the château's page reference.

CHER

Béthune
La Chapelle d'Angillon
Open daily except Sunday morning from Palm Sunday to October.
Guided visits include audio-visual show (10 mins) about Alain-Fournier, author of *Le Grand Meaulnes*, born in La Chapelle d'Angillon, and for whom the château inspired his celebrated novel.
Tel: (48)73 41 10

Blancafort
Open daily except Tuesday, mid-April to October; and Sunday afternoon, November to December.
Guided visits (30 mins). Pamphlets in English.
Tel: (48)58 60 56

Boucard
Jars-le-Noyer. 5km south of Jars on D74.
Open daily all year. Pamphlets in English.
Tel: (48)58 72 81

Palais Jacques Coeur
Bourges, Rue Jacques Coeur.
Open daily.
Tel: (48)24 06 87

Maupas
Morogues. ¾km west on D59.
Open daily July to early September; mornings only mid-April to June and early September to mid-October.
Tel: (48)64 41 71

Mehun-sur-Yèvre
Open daily except Tuesdays July to August. Mornings only last three weeks in June and first two weeks in September (closed Tuesday), and open all day Sunday.
Tel: (48)57 30 25

Menetou-Salon
Open each morning last week in April to November. Pamphlets in English.
Tel: (48)64 80 54 or 64 80 16

La Verrerie
Oizon. D39 south of Oizon for 6km; left after Les Naudins for 1km on D89.
Open daily mid-February to mid-November.
Tel: (48)58 06 91

INDRE

Châtillon-sur-Indre
Apply to porter at château.

Valençay
Guided visits (60 mins) daily 10 March to 18 November. Pamphlets in English. Entrance charge includes gardens and Musée de l'Automobile du Centre (60 vintage cars dating from 1898).
Tel: (54)00 10 66

INDRE-ET-LOIRE

Amboise
Guided visits (30 mins) daily all year.
Tel: (47)57 00 98

Azay-le-Rideau
Open daily all year. Pamphlets in English.
Tel: (47)43 32 04

Bridoré
Open afternoons mid-June to August.

Chatigny
Fondettes. On D76, right at Mareuil on D276, and first right. Open daily all year to see exterior only.
Tel: (47)42 20 05

Chenonceau
Open daily all year. Snack bar, tea rooms. Children's nursery July to August. Electric train in July and August. Pamphlets in English. Musée de Cire (Waxwork Museum) in grounds of château, with wax models to illustrate history and personalities connected with château. Open daily all year.
Tel: (47)29 90 07 or 29 93 52

Chinon
Open daily February to November; closed Wednesday rest of year. Pamphlets in

English. Ticket gives access to Fort St Georges, Château du Milieu, Fort du Coudray. For Logis Royaux guided visits (30 mins) only.
Tel: (47)93 13 45

Cinq Mars-la-Pile
Open daily except Monday 1 March to 11 November. Pamphlets in English. Guided visits (30 mins) including park.
Tel: (47)96 40 49

Langeais
Open daily all year except Monday out of season. In summer, closed Monday morning. Audio-commentaries in each of the furnished apartments. Pamphlets in English.
Tel: (47)96 72 60

Leugny
Azay-sur-Cher. 2km east of Azay on N76, and left along drive.
Guided tours in afternoons from last week in July to August. At other times, groups by previous arrangement.
Tel: (47)50 41 10

Loches
Logis Royal. Open daily February to November; closed Wednesday out of season. Includes Tour Agnès Sorel, Logis Royaux tomb of Agnès Sorel, triptych of School of Jean Fouquet (fifteenth century). Pamphlets in English.
Tel: (47)59 01 32

Loches
Guided visits to donjon (keep) daily February to November; closed Wednesday out of season. Visit includes Tour Ronde and Martelet. Pamphlets in English.
Tel: (47)50 07 86

Montpoupon
Montrichard. 12km south-west from Montrichard on D764.
Open daily mid-June to September; afternoon only first three weeks in April; Saturday and Sunday afternoons only last week in April to mid-June, and October.
Tel: (47)94 23 62

Montrésor
Guided visits (30 mins) daily April to October. Pamphlets in English.
Tel: (47)94 20.04

Nitray
Athée-sur-Cher. 2km north of Athée.
Open daily July to mid-August.
Tel: (47)50 68 07

Plessis-lès-Tours
Guided visits (45 mins) daily except Tuesday and public holidays, February to December. Pamphlets in English.
Tel: (47)61 51 87 or 05 68 73

Réaux
Bourgueil. South on D749 for 4km to Les Réaux, right to far end of village.
Group visits by previous arrangement.
Tel: (47)95 14 40

Rivau
Champigny-sur-Veude. 4km north on D749 to Le Coudray, first left off D114.
Guided visits (90 mins) daily mid-March to October.
Tel: Paris (1)245 63 57

La Roche Racan
St Paterne Racan. 1.5km south-east on D28.
Guided visits August to mid-September.

Saché
Open daily February to November; closed Wednesday February to mid-March, and October to November. Pamphlets in English.
Tel: (47)26 86 50

Ste Maure-de-Touraine
Open daily except Sunday mid-June to mid-September. At other times groups by previous arrangement. Commentaries in English.
Tel: (47)65 66 35

Ussé
Rigny-Ussé.
Guided visits (45 mins) daily mid-March to November. Pamphlets in English.
Tel: (47)95 54 05

Vaudésir Manoir
St Christophe-sur-le-Nais.
Open daily all year except Monday.
Tel: (47)29 24 53

Villandry
Guided visits (30 mins) daily of interior of château, mid-March to mid-November. Commentaries in English. (For garden, see 'Wild Life, Zoos and Gardens'.)
Tel: (47)50 02 09

LOIR-ET-CHER
Beauregard
Cellettes. Just north of village.
Open daily all year, but closed Wednesdays early February to March and October to December. Guided visits (30 mins). Pamphlets in English. Includes

Galerie des Illustres (historical portraits), *Cabinet des Grelots* (sixteenth-century room) and sixteenth-century kitchen.
Tel: (54)44 20 05

Blois
Open daily all year. Guided visits (45 mins) in English available. Audio-visual performances in season. Entrance charge includes St Saturnin cemetery, Musée des Beaux Arts, Musée Archéologique.
Tel: (54)78 06 62 or 74 16 06

Chambord
Open daily January to December. Pamphlets in English.
Tel: (54)46 31 32 or 78 19 47

Chaumont-sur-Loire
Open daily January to December. Guided visits (30 mins) include stables and park. Park alone can be visited.
Tel: (54)78 19 47 and 46 98 03

Chémery
Furnished apartments open daily all year. Commentaries (30 mins) and pamphlets in English.
Tel: (54)71 82 77

Cheverny
Cour-Cheverny. Open daily all year. Guided tours available. Pamphlets in English.
Tel: (54)79 96 29

La Ferté-Imbault
Open afternoons Monday, Saturday, Sunday, July to September. Commentaries (45 mins) in English.
Tel: Paris (1)622 47 26

Fougères-sur-Bièvre
Open daily all year except Tuesday and Wednesday and public holidays. 30 mins.
Tel: (54)78 19 47 or 46 27 18

Gué-Péan
Monthou-sur-Cher. East of village along 1km drive.
Guided visits (45 mins) of furnished rooms daily all year. Commentaries in English.
Tel: (54)71 43 01

Lavardin
Guided visits (60 mins) of ruins daily during school holidays of Easter and summer.
Tel: Paris (1)508 80 40

Ménars
Temporarily closed at time of writing.
Tel: (54)46 81 27 or 46 81 55

Montoire-sur-le-Loir
Square keep of eleventh century. Apply to Syndicat d'Initiative, Mairie (Tel: (54)85 00 29) which is open daily except Sunday, July to mid-September, for arrangement to view. Model of original château in Mairie.

Montrichard
Keep open daily early June to early September, and Saturday and Sunday only mid-April to early June, mid-September to November. 35 mins. Pamphlets in English.
Tel: (54)32 05 10

Le Moulin
Lassay-sur-Croisne. 1.5km west of Lassay. Guided tours (30 mins) daily March to mid-November.
Tel: (54)83 83 51

St Denis-sur-Loire
Open daily except Sunday January to September to view exterior only.
Tel: (54)78 31 02

Selles-sur-Cher
Open daily July to mid-September, and afternoons of Saturday and Sunday mid-September to June. Closed mid-November to Easter.
Tel: (54)97 59 10

Talcy
Guided visits (30 mins) daily except Tuesday, January to December includes furnished apartments and their tapestries, pigeon-loft, and 400-year-old wine press.
Tel: (54)78 19 47

Troussay
Cour-Cheverny. D52 southwest of Cour-Cheverny, right fork in 3km. Guided visits (25 mins) daily last week in March to mid-April, and May to mid-September; Sunday and public holidays only last two weeks in April and mid-September to mid-November. Includes collection of traditional agricultural implements of Sologne.
Tel: (54)79 96 07 or Paris (1)288 71 28

Vendôme
Open daily July to August; daily except Tuesday March to April, and September to November; Sunday afternoons only, January to February and December. Separate charges for château and gardens.
Tel: (54)77 01 33

Villesavin
Bracieux. 3km west of Bracieux on D102, right at Ponts-d'Arian, cross river Beuvron, right along drive. Guided visits (45 mins) daily March to September, and afternoons only October to mid-December. Pamphlets in English. Tel: (54)46 42 88

LOIRET
Beaugency
Château Dunois. Guided visits (45 mins) daily all year, but closed Tuesday out of season except to parties by previous arrangement. Includes Musée Régional des Arts et Traditions de l'Orléanais. Tel: (38)44 55 23

Châteauneuf-sur-Loire
Daily visits all year to view exterior and gardens, arboretum, giant rhododendrons. Tel: (38)58 41 18

Gien
Guided visits (60 mins) daily all year, includes Musée International de la Chasse (museum of the history of hunting). Tel: (38)67 24 11

Le Lude
La Ferté-St Aubin. West on D61 from La Ferté, lane off right for 1km. Open daily mid-January to October, exterior only. Tel: Paris (1)651 73 50
Not to be confused with *son-et-lumière* château of Le Lude in Sarthe.

Meung-sur-Loire
Guided visits (60 mins) in English daily April to mid-September; Saturday and Sunday only January to March and mid-September to December. At other times groups by previous arrangement. Entrance charges for both château and undergound oubliettes. Tel: (38)44 36 47 or 44 25 61

Orléans
Hôtel Groslot, Place de l'Etape. Open daily all year. Pamphlets in English. Tel: (38)42 22 22

Sully-sur-Loire
Guided visits (45 mins) daily March to November. Tel: (38)62 04 88

MAINE-ET-LOIRE
Anger
Open daily all year except public holidays. Entrance fee includes access to Musée Lurçat, Musée des Beaux-Arts, Musée Pincé and cathedral treasury. Pamphlets in English. Tel: (41)87 43 47

Baugé
Château du Roi René. Open daily June to September. Tel: (41)89 18 07

Boumois
St Martin-de-la-Place. 1km south-east of St Martin, off D952. Open daily except Tuesday, Easter to All Saints' Day. Tel: (41)51 35 50

Coudray-Montbault
St Hilaire-du-Bois. 3km north-west on D254 beyond crossroads with N160. Open daily July to mid-September. Tel: (41)64 80 47

Brissac
Guided visits (60 mins) daily July to August; daily except Tuesday early February to June and September to mid-November. Tel: (41)91 23 43

Manoir de la Harmonière
Champigné. D768 south for 1.5km, left. Open daily July to mid-September. Tel: (41)42 01 38

Lathan
Breil. D86 south-east of Breil of 0.5km. Enquire at château for authorisation to visit.

La Lorie
Segré. 2km south of Segré on D961. Guided visits (30 mins) afternoons July to mid-September; closed Tuesday. Pamphlets in English. Tel: (41)92 10 04

Montgeoffroy
Mazé. 2km north-west of Mazé on D74. Open daily Palm Sunday to All Saints' Day. Tel: (41)80 60 02

Montreuil-Bellay
Guided visits (45 mins) daily except Tuesday April to October and daily including Tuesday afternoon July to August. Commentaries in English. Gardens alone can be visited. Tel: (41)52 33 06

Montsoreau
Guided visits (60 mins) daily except Tuesday all year. Tel: (41)51 70 25

La Perrière
Avrillé. From Angers on N162, right at
Avrillé for 0.5km. Open daily except
Wednesday July to mid-September.
Tel: (41)69 20 17

Le Plessis-Bourré
Ecuillé. D74 west from Ecuillé, right on
D508 for 1.5km. Guided visits (45 mins)
daily all year except Wednesday and
Sunday morning.
Tel: (41)91 66 25

Le Plessis-Macé
Guided visits (60 mins) daily except
Tuesday July to September; at other times
afternoons only. Closed October to
February.

Les Ponts-de-Cé
Open daily except Monday April to
September.

Raguin
Chazé-sur-Argos. Just north of village.
Open daily mid-May to mid-September
afternoon only.
Tel: (41)92 13 62

Serrant
St Georges-sur-Loire. N23 towards
Angers, right in 1km. Guided visits (45
mins) daily April to October. Closed
Tuesday except July and August; furnished
apartments included.
Tel: (41)41 13 01

Saumur
Open daily April to October, and daily
except Tuesday, November to March.
Guided visits (60 mins) in English.
Entrance fee includes Musée des Arts
Decoratifs and Musée du Cheval.
Tel: (41)51 30 46

SARTHE
Bazouges-sur-le Loir
Open Saturday afternoon from Easter
Saturday to June; Tuesday morning,
Thursday and Saturday afternoon, July to
mid-September.
Tel: (43)94 30 67

Courtanvaux
Bessé-sur-Braye. 1km north of Bessé.
Open daily, May to September at 10, 11am
and 2, 3, 4, 5, 6pm when there are at least
six persons in a group. Closed Tuesday.
Rest of year, open Sundays and public
holidays at the same times. In summer, art
exhibitions, concerts, plays.

Poncé-sur-le-Loir
Open daily all year except Sunday
morning, for visit of château, gardens,
pigeon-loft.
Tel: (43)44 45 31

La Possonnière
Couture-sur-Loir. Manor house lies 0.5km
south of Couture.
Private property, but grounds of birthplace
of poet Ronsard may be visited during
absence of owners, and by prior
arrangement.

MUSEUMS AND BUILDINGS OF SPECIAL INTEREST

For information about opening days and
times see introduction to 'Châteaux open
to the public'.

CHER
Bourges
Cathedral crypt and tower
Audio-visual '*Trésors d'Art du Cher*', daily
except Sunday morning, last week in April
to October.

Musée du Berry
Hôtel Cujas, 4 Rue des Arènes.
Tel: (48)70 41 92
Social history, archaeology of province.
Open daily except Tuesday, and New
Year's Day.

Hôtel Lallemant
6 Rue Bourbonnoux.
Tel: (48)70 19 32
Art collection.
Open daily except Monday, 2 January to
31 December.

Museum d'Histoire Naturelle
Rue Messire Jacques.
Tel: (48)70 19 82
Natural history collections.
Open all year, afternoon only Wednesday
to Sunday.

Guided tours of old quarters, starting at
Office de Tourisme, 14 Place E. Dolet.
Tel: (48)24 75 33
Pamphlets in English.

Nançay
Observatoire de Radioastronomie
Radio-astronomy centre. Commentaries in
English.
Open daily all year to groups by previous
arrangement.

Grenier de Villâtre
Exhibition of work by group of artists.
Open Saturdays and Sundays.

Vierzon
Musée des Amis du Vieux Vierzon
Rue du Château.
Tel: (48)71 47 86
Porcelain exhibition.

INDRE
Chabris
Mairie
Tel: (54)40 03 32
Collections of insects and old coins.
Open Sunday afternoon, July to August.

Luçay-le-Mâle
Musée de la Pierre à Fusil
Village de Retraite, Rue du Champ de
Foire.
Tel: (54)40 45 61 or 40 43 97
Flintlock collection.

INDRE-ET-LOIRE
Amboise
Musée de l'Hôtel de Ville
Rue François I.
Tel: (47)57 02 21
Local history and paintings.
Open all year on Saturday and Sunday,
and on all other days by previous
arrangement.

Musée de la Poste
Hôtel de Joyeuse, 6 Rue de Joyeuse.
Tel: (47)57 00 11
History of early postal services.
Open daily except Tuesday and public
holidays.

Manoir de Clos-Lucé
Rue du Clos-Lucé.
Tel: (47)57 62 88
Manor house, gardens, Leonardo da Vinci
museum with working models of his
inventions. Pamphlets in English.
Open daily February to December.

Pagode de Chanteloup
2.5km south on Bléré road.
Folly in Chinese style, grounds, woods.
Pamphlets in English.
Open daily except Monday all year.

Avoine
Centrale Nucléaire de Chinon
Tel: (47)93 04 50
Chinon nuclear power station.
Commentary in English. Viewing platform
open daily all year.

Open all year Monday to Friday to groups
by previous arrangement (minimum
notice, two weeks).

Bourgueil
Benedictine Abbey.
Tel: (47)97 72 04
Guided tours from Easter to September on
Sunday afternoon and public holidays, as
well as Friday to Monday, July to August
(60 mins).

Champigny-sur-Veude
Chapelle du Château
Tel: (47)95 73 20
Commentaries (45 mins) in English.
Groups by previous arrangement daily for
rest of year. Sixteenth-century stained glass
windows.
Open daily April to early November.

Chinon
Musée du Vieux Chinon
Maison des Etats Généraux, 44 Rue Haute
St Maurice.
Tel: (47)93 17 85
Museum of local curios.
Open daily except Tuesday and January
and February.

Musée des Arts et Traditions Populaires
Chapelle Ste Radegonde.
Tel: (47)93 17 85
Guided visits by previous arrangement
daily, June to mid-August. Commentaries
in English.

Musée des Voitures Hippomobiles
La Cave aux Bussards, Route d'Avoine.
Tel: (47)61 08 94
Exhibition of horse-carriages by river
Vienne.
Open Saturday and Sunday (groups by
previous arrangement on weekdays) April
to September.

Tour of old town, starting from Office de
Tourisme, Place Général de Gaulle.
Tel: (47)93 17 85
Daily May to September. Groups by
previous arrangement during rest of year.

La Devinière
Cross river Vienne by D749, right on
D751, left in 3km on D759 and right on
D117.
Tel: (47)93 13 45
Birthplace of Rabelais and museum.
Pamphlets in English.
Open daily except Wednesday and January
and February.

Cormery
Abbey.

Tel: (47)43 42 52
Only remains of cloisters can be visited.

Cravant-les-Coteaux
Musée du Vieux-Cravant
Mairie.
Tel: (47)93 12 40
Lapidary museum.
Open afternoons only (closed Tuesday) all
year.

L'Ile-Bouchard
Prieuré St Léonard
Apply to house next door to see carved
capitals on four columns in twelfth-century
church.

Loches
Nocturnal tour of old town, starting from
Pavillon du Tourisme, Place Marne.
Tel: (47)59 07 98
At 9.30pm daily, July to mid-September.
Commentaries in English. Groups by
previous arrangement daily during rest of
year.

Musée Lansyer et Musée du Terroir
Rue Lansyer.
Tel: (47)59 05 45
Reconstructed Touraine house of
nineteenth century, local costumes, arms,
historical objects.
Open daily except Friday. Guided visits
July to mid-September.

Abbey church at Beaulieu-lès-Loches, 1km
east.
Apply to Mairie for guided tours in
summer. Or ask for key at 2 Rue Foulques
Nerra.

Luzé
Abbaye de Bois Aubry
Twelfth-century Benedictine abbey, 3km
south-east of Luzé, left off D110.
Tel: (47)58 34 48
Open daily all year except during services.
Commentaries in English.

Meslay
Parçay-Meslay, medieval tithe barn.
Tel: (47)51 31 21
Audio-visual show, '*Un pilier de la grange
raconte. . . .*' Pamphlets in English. Art
exhibitions, auditorium for Touraine
Music Festival (last weekend in June, first
weekend in July). Open afternoon only,

Saturday, Sunday and public holidays, late
April to October.

Montrésor
Chartreuse du Liget
6km west of Montrésor on D760.
Tel: (47)94 20 02
Exterior only can be viewed daily. To see
over Carthusian buildings (privately
owned) enquire at door on left of main
courtyard.

Chapelle St Jean du Liget
6.5km west of Montrésor on D760, left
along lane and right along rough track.
To obtain key to twelfth-century circular
chapel, ask at Chartreuse du Liget (above).

Négron
2km west of Amboise on N152.
Twelfth-century barn. Art exhibitions in
summer.

Richelieu
Musée de l'Hôtel de Ville.
Tel: (47)58 10 13
History of town.
Open daily except Tuesday and Sunday,
January to June; daily except Tuesday,
July to August; daily except Tuesday and
Sunday, September to December.

St Etienne-de-Chigny
11km west of Tours on N152, right.
Sixteenth-century church with huge carved
grotesque masks on timbers, stained glass
windows. Key obtainable at grocery
(closed Mondays) next door.

Savigné-sur-Lathan
Musée des Faluns Savignéens
Faubourg de la Rue.
Tel: (47)24 60 19
Geology museum. Pamphlets in English.
Open Saturday and Sunday afternoons,
mid-March to June and September to mid-
November; open every afternoon except
Thursday, July to August.

Savonnières
Caves Pétrifiantes
Tel: (47)50 00 09
Petrified caves. Pamphlets in English.
Guided visits (45 mins) daily except
Thursday, March and mid-September to
December; daily April to mid-September.

Tavant Church
2km outside L'Ile-Bouchard, west on

D760, narrow turning on left in village. To view twelfth-century frescoes, apply to address given on notice-board outside church.

Tours
Daily audio-guided tour round old quarters from Office de Tourisme, Place Maréchal Leclerc. Tapes in English.
Tel: (47)05 58 08

Visit to old quarters with English-speaking guide available daily all year by previous arrangement.
Tel: (47)61 61 23

Musée des Equipages Militaires et du Train
Rue du Plat d'Etain.
Tel: (47)61 44 46
Museum of the history of military baggae-trains.
Open all year, afternoons only, Monday to Friday. On Saturday and Sunday open to groups by previous arrangement.

Hôtel Mame
19 Rue Emile Zola.
Tel: (47)05 60 87
Exhibition of silks produced by one-time Tours factories. Pamphlets in English.
Open afternoons only, April to mid-November.

Musée de Compagnonnage
Cloître St Julien, 8 Rue Nationale.
Tel: (47)61 07 93
Museum of ancient crafts and tools used by organised *compagnons* (guilds) of craftsmen. Pamphlets in English.
Open daily all year except Tuesday and public holidays.

Musée des Vins de Touraine
Celliers St Julien, 16 Rue Nationale.
Tel: (47)61 07 93
Museum of history of every aspect of wine. Pamphlets in English.
Open daily all year except Tuesday and public holidays.

Musée Archéologique de Touraine
Hôtel Goüin, 25 Rue du Commerce.
Tel: (47)66 22 32
Museum of regional archaeology. Pamphlets in English.
Open daily except Friday, February to mid-March, and October to November; open daily mid-March to September.

Musée du Gemmail
Hôtel Rimbaud, 7 Rue du Mûrier.

Tel: (47)61 01 19
Museum of pictorial reproductions by modern techniques.
Open daily except Monday, mid-April to mid-October.

Musée des Beaux-Arts
18 Place François-Picard.
Tel: (47)05 68 73
Art gallery.
Open daily except Tuesday, late January to March and October to December; open daily April to September. Closed on public holidays.

Château Royal
Quai d'Orléans. Historial de la Touraine, Musée de Cires.
Tel: (47)66 75 92
Waxworks museum
Open daily April to October; open afternoons only November to December.

Cloître St Gatien (La Psalette)
Attached to north side of cathedral.
Guided tours daily. Apply to cathedral caretaker.

St Cosme Priory
Plessis-lès-Tours, 3km west of centre of Tours on south side of Loire.
Tel: (47)20 99 29
Tomb of poet Ronsard. Pamphlets in English.
Open daily except Wednesday February to mid-March and October to November; daily mid-March to September.

Turpenay Abbey
In Forêt de Chinon. From Chinon, D751 towards Azay-le-Rideau; left after 8km, through St Benoît-la-Forêt and right after 2km.
Tel: (47)58 01 47
Exterior only open all day throughout year, Monday to Friday. Pamphlets in English.

Villaines-les-Rochers
Société Coopérative Agricole de Vannerie.
Tel: (47)43 33 03
Exhibition and sale of long-established local basket-work industry.

LOIR-ET-CHER
Blois
Musée Lapidaire
Cloître St Saturnin, Rue Munier.
Tel: (54)78 06 62 or 74 10 06
Museum of sculpture.
Open all day Wednesday, Saturday,

Sunday January to mid-March and
November to December; all day
Wednesday to Sunday mid-March to
October. Ticket admits to château.

Hôtel d'Alluye
Italian Renaissance courtyard and galleries
can be visited during office hours.

Chocolaterie Poulain
To arrange visit to factory (75 mins) Tel:
(54)78 39 21 extension 339.

Visits to old quarters '*Blois historique*'
from Office de Tourisme, Pavillon Anne de
Bretagne, 3 Avenue Jean Laigret.
Tel: (54)74 06 49 or 78 23 21
Daily except Wednesday and Sunday, July
and August. Groups daily during rest of
year by previous arrangement.

La Chaussée-St Victor
Musée Adrien Thiebault
116 Rue Nationale, on eastern outskirts of
Blois.
Small museum of naive ceramics, dolls and
models reconstructing local scenes.

Gy-en-Sologne
Locature de la Straize.
13km west of Romorantin-Lanthenay on
D59.
Tel: (54)83 82 89
Agricultural museum.
Open daily except Saturday and Sunday,
mid-March to mid-November.

Lassay-sur-Croisne
11km west of Romorantin-Lanthenay on
D59 and D20.
Fifteenth-century church with sixteenth-
century frescoes. Enquire at town hall.

Lanthenay
Enquire for key at house opposite Calvary
on D922, to see sixteenth-century paintings
and wooden statues in the church.

Maves
Moulin-à-vent.
17km along Blois to Châteaudun road,
D924, right on D112.
Tel: (54)81 31 35
Windmill open Sunday afternoon mid-
March to mid-November. Groups by
previous arrangement, Monday to
Saturday, mid-March to mid-November.

Mennetou-sur-Cher
Thirteenth-century church. Apply to town
hall.

Meusnes
Musée de la Pierre à fusil
Mairie, 7km south-west of Selles-sur-Cher,
on D956 and D17.
Tel: (54)71 00 23
Flint knapping museum.
Open Sunday afternoon July to August, or
by previous arrangement on Tuesday to
Saturday, January to June, and September
to December, and Monday to Saturday,
July to August.

Montoire-sur-le-Loir
Chapelle St Gilles
Open daily all year. Twelfth-century
murals.

Neuvy-sur-Beuvron
Apply to house facing church to see
fifteenth-century statues and seventeenth-
century painting.

Oisly
'*La Presle*', *Souvenirs de l'Agriculture et de
la Viticulture anciennes*
3km south of Contres on D675, right on
D21 for 3km.
Tel: (54)79 52 69
Museum of traditional agricultural and
viticultural techniques.
Open Tuesday and Saturday afternoon,
mid-June to mid-September.

Pontlevoy
Ancienne abbaye
Guided visits (45 mins) daily, July to mid-
September; afternoons only April to June.
Closed on Monday.

Romorantin-Lanthenay
Visit to old quarters from Syndicat
d'Initiative, Place Paix.
Tel: (54)76 43 89
Groups by previous arrangement daily
January to June and September to
December; individual visitors Saturday
mornings only, July and August.

Musée de Sologne
Hôtel de Ville, Faubourg St Roch.
Tel: (54)76 07 06
Museum of local ethnology.
Open daily except Tuesday all year.

Musée Municipal de la Course Automobile
29-31 Faubourg d'Orléans.
Tel: (54)76 07 06
Racing car museum.
Open daily all year except Tuesday and
Sunday morning.

Musée Archéologique M. de Marcheville
Le Carroir Doré, La Chancellerie, 14 Rue
de la Résistance.
Tel: (54)76 22 06 or 76 31 10 (mornings)
Private archaeological collection.
Open daily all year by previous
arrangement.

St Laurent-Nouan
Centrale Nucléaire St Laurent A & B
Nuclear Power Station.
Tel: (54)78 52 52
Observation platform, small exhibition
room and information centre open daily all
year. Visit to power station (150 mins) by
previous arrangement (two months' notice
in writing), Monday to Friday all year.

Selles-sur-Cher
*Musée municipal d'Histoire et de Traditions
Locales.*
Cloître de l'Ancienne Abbaye.
Tel: (54)97 40 19
Museum of local history and traditions.
Open Saturday and Sunday, and Tuesday
and Thursday morning, July and August.
At other times by previous arrangement.

Talcy
Moulin à vent
Tel: (54)81 03 03 or 81 20 45
Windmill open Sunday afternoon only,
May to mid-October.

Thésée-la-Romaine
Musée des Fouilles
Le Vaulx-St Georges.
Tel: (54)71 40 20
Museum of local Roman excavations.
Open each afternoon except Tuesday, July
and August.

Troo
Grotte Pétrifiante
Stalactites and petrified objects in cave.
Parking nearby.
Open daily, April to September.

Vendôme
Tour of old quarters from Office de
Tourisme, Rue Poterie.
Tel: (54)77 05 07
Groups by previous arrangement daily all
year. Commentaries and pamphlets in
English.

Musée Municipal
Cloître de la Trinité.
Tel: (54)77 26 13

Religious art of Vendômois, period
furniture, faience chinaware, musical
instruments, prehistory, tools of ancient
regional trades.
Open daily all year except Tuesday.

LOIRET
Beaugency
Tour of old quarters from Château
Dunois.
Tel: (38)44 55 23
Groups by previous arrangement daily all
year.

Hôtel de Ville
Tel: (38)44 50 01
Collection of embroideries and Gobelin
tapestries.
Open daily all year except Wednesday.

Aquarium
2 Promenade de Barchelin.
Tel: (38)44 81 69
Exotic fish.
Open daily July to August, and daily
except Tuesday January to June and
September to December.

La Chapelle-St Mesmin
Grotte 'du Dragon'
Western outskirts of Orléans on N152.
Tel: (38)72 60 03
Restored grotto of St Mesmin underneath
chapel.
Open daily all year by previous
arrangement.

Châteauneuf-sur-Loire
*Musée de la Marine de Loire et du Vieux
Châteauneuf.*
History of navigation on Loire.
Open daily except Tuesday, June to
August; Sunday afternoon in April, May,
September.

Chécy
Musée de la Tonnellerie
1 Avenue de Patay, 10km east of Orléans,
off N60.
Tel: (38)62 72 45
Cooperage museum. Pamphlets in English.
Open Sunday afternoon, July to
September; daily in June by previous
arrangement.

Cléry-St André
15km south-west of Orléans on D951,
Basilique.
Tel: (38)45 70 05
Basilica open daily all year. To visit vault

and oratory of Louis XI, and Chapelle St Jacques, apply to sacristan or presbytery, 1 Rue du Cloître.

Dampierre-en-Burly
Centrale Nucléaire
13km north-west of Gien on D952. Information centre of nuclear power station open weekdays and Saturday, Sunday and public holidays afternoons. Guided visits last about 3 hours including 75 mins of films, and tour of station, by previous arrangement.

Germiny-des-Prés
Carolingian Oratory
4.5km south-east of Châteauneuf-sur-Loire on D60.
Tel: (38)58 27 97
Open daily all year. Commentaries in English available. Pamphlets in English. Parking outside.

Gien
Musée et Salle d'Exposition de la Faïencerie
Place de la Victoire, on D952 in north-west suburb of Gien.
Guided visits at 9.30, 10.30am, 2.30, 3.30pm daily except Saturday, Sunday and public holidays. Displays of old pieces of Gien pottery in museum; pottery in current production in *Salle d'Exposition*. To see over factory tel: (38)67 00 05; no children under 12 years.

Jargeau
Musée 'Le Médailleur Oscar Roty et son temps'
3 Place du Petit Cloître.
Tel: Paris (1)222 24 96
Collection of sculpture, medals, coins in home of engraver Roty.
Open Saturday afternoon and all day Sunday, June to September.

Meung-sur-Loire
Musée Gaston Couté
Mairie.
Tel: (38)44 42 88
Souvenirs of Montmartre song-writer. Museum being reorganised at time of writing.

Orléans
Tour of old quarters from Maison de Tourisme, Place Albert I.
Tel: (38)53 05 95
Mid-July to mid-September at 3pm;

commentaries in English. At other times of year groups by previous arrangement.

Musée Historique et Archéologique de l'Orléanais
Hôtel Cabu, Place Abbé Desnoyers.
Tel: (38)53 39 22
Prehistory and antiquity.
Open daily all year except Tuesday and public holidays.

Maison Jeanne d'Arc
Place du Général de Gaulle.
Tel: (38)42 22 69
Exhibits related to Joan of Arc and her times.
Open afternoon only, Tuesday to Sunday, January to April and November to December; daily except Monday, May to October.

Hôtel Toutin
Inner courtyard of sixteenth-century mansion at any time except Sunday, Monday and month of August.

Musée des Sciences Naturelles
2 Rue Marcel Proust.
Tel: (38)42 25 58
Natural history museum open all day Wednesday and Sunday and afternoons only Monday, Tuesday, Thursday, Friday all year.

Musée des Beaux-Arts
Hôtel des Crénaux, Place de la République.
Open daily all year except Tuesday.

Cathedral of Ste Croix
Tel: (38)53 47 23
Open daily all year. Guided visits of choir, crypt and treasury between 2 and 6pm in season. Pamphlets in English.

Collégiale St Aignan
Also crypt of St Avit.
Tel: (38)66 24 10
Open all year to groups by previous arrangement. Commentaries in English.

St Benoît-sur-Loire
Abbaye de Fleury
Tel: (38)35 72 43
Open daily all year except Saturday morning and all Sunday, outside times of services. Guided visits daily except Saturday morning and Sunday, May to September. Commentaries and pamphlets in English. Gregorian chant sung at Mass on Sunday and certain public holidays at

10.45am, and on weekdays at 11.45am.

Tigy
Musée de l'Artisanat Rural Ancien
60 Rue de Sully, 8km south of
Châteauneuf-sur-Loire on D11.
Tel: (38)58 00 42
Museum of ancient crafts. Commentaries
in English.
Open Sunday afternoon, late April to mid-
October; open daily for rest of year to
groups by previous arrangement.

Vienne-en-Val
Salles d'Exposition Archéologique
Route de Tigy, 7.5km south of Jargeau on
D12.
Tel: (38)58 81 24
Archaeological museum open Sunday
afternoon, April to November.

MAINE-ET-LOIRE
Anger
Single ticket gives access to four buildings
below marked *, as well as to the Château
(see under 'Châteaux open to the Public').

Musée Jean Lurçat
4 Boulevard Arago.
Tel: (41)87 41 06
Tapestries by Jean Lurçat and medieval
hospital ward and dispensary.
Open daily all year except Monday and
public holidays.

Musée des Beaux-Arts
Logis Barrault, Rue du Musée.
Noted for complete collection of plaster
casts by sculptor David d'Angers, as well
as paintings of nineteenth-century French
school.
Open daily except Monday and public
holidays.

Cathedral Treasury
Open daily except Sunday and Monday,
April to June; daily July to September; all
day for rest of year from Tuesday to
Saturday. Closed on public holidys.

Musée Turpin de Crissé
Hôtel Pincé, Rue Lenepveu.
Japanese and Chinese ceramics; Egyptian
collection; Greek and Etruscan vases.
Open daily except Monday and public
holidays.

Préfecture
To visit seventeenth-century buildings and
Romanesque cloisters, apply to porter.

Baugé
Hôpital St Joseph
Seventeeth-century hospital and
dispensary.
Open daily except Thursday morning. To
see over building, enquire at reception
office.

Chapelle des Filles du Coeur de Marie
Contains Croix d'Anjou.
Open all weekdays and Sunday afternoon.
Ring doorbell of Community, 8 Rue de la
Girouardière.

Beaulieu-sur-Layon
Caveau du Vin
Exhibition of old Anjou wine bottles and
glasses.
Open daily all year.

La Boissière Abbey
10km south of Le Lude on D307.
Open daily early August to early
September, late December to January.

La Bourgonnière Chapel
6km west of St Florent-le-Viel on D751.
Open daily all year.

Dénezé-sous-Doué
Cavernes sculptés
5.5km north of Doué-la-Fontaine on D69.
Hundreds of grotesque and erotic carvings
on walls of cave, dating from sixteenth
century.
Open daily all year except December and
January.

Doué-la-Fontaine
Quartier de Douces, Arènes.
Guided visits (30 mins) of quarries whose
arena-like seats were carved in fifteenth
century. Now used for concerts, plays and
flower shows.
Open all year except Tuesday out of
season.

Fontevraud-l'Abbaye
Guided visits daily all year except Tuesday
and public holidays, of church, cloisters,
refectory, huge Romanesque kitchens.
Abbey houses *Centre Culturel de Rencontre*
of *Centre Culturel de l'Ouest*, where
concerts, exhibitions, conferences are held.
Information on programmes, tel: (41)51 73
52 or 51 71 82.

Jarzé
Chapelle Notre Dame-de-Montplacé

2km north-east of Jarzé on D82, then right.
Key to solitary and simple chapel at Maison des Religieuses, near Jarzé church.

Linières-Bouton
South on D767 from Noyant for 7km, right, and right again for village.
To see Plantagenent choir and seventeenth-century painting of Annunciation in church, ask for key at grocer's shop, Place de l'Eglise.

Liré
Musée Joachim du Bellay
Small museum of mementoes of sixteenth-century Angevin poet.
Tel: (40)83 24 13
Open daily except Monday.

Louresse-Rochemenier
Musée Paysan
6.5km north-west of Doué-la-Fontaine on D761.
Tel: (41)59 13 13
Peasant museum of old farm implements, costumes in cave, illustrating how peasants used to cultivate crops underground (45 mins).
Open daily except Monday, April to September; in July and August also open Monday; open afternoons Saturday, Sunday and public holidays rest of year except December and January.

Montreuil-Bellay
Ancienne Abbaye d'Asnières
5.5km on D761 towards Doué-la-Fontaine, right at Brossay for 2km.
Guided visits (30 mins) of ruins of twelfth-century abbey and choir in Gothic Angevin style, daily July and August.

St Aubin-de-Luigné
Château de la Haute-Guerche
4km south of Rochefort-sur-Loire on D54, 1km west on D125.
Ruined fortress with wide views.
Open daily July and August.

Saumur
Musée d'Arts Décoratifs and *Musée du Cheval*
Museum of Decorative Arts in Château contains varied collection of medieval and Renaissance decorative works; Horse Museum presents history of riding.
Open daily except Tuesday.

Musée de la Cavalerie
Avenue Maréchal Foch.
Guided visits daily all year except August.

Musée des Blindés
Armoured vehicle museum open daily all year.

École Nationale d'Equitation
St Hilaire-St Florent, western suburb on south bank of Loire on D751.
Guided visits round National Riding School for minimum of ten persons arranged at Office de Tourisme, 25 Rue Beaurepaire, Tel: (41)51 03 06

Musée du Champignon
St Hilaire-St Florent.
Tel: (41)50 31 55
Guided visits daily mid-March to mid-November round cliff caves where techniques of growing different varieties of mushroom are shown.

Dolmen de Bagneux
2km south on N147, left by church on D160.
Apply to Café-Restaurant du Dolmen (drinks obligatory) for entrance to enclosure to see one of France's largest megalithic monuments.

St Laurent-de-la-Plaine
Musée des Vieux Métiers
5km south-west of Chalonnes on D762.
Tel: (41)78 24 08
Craftsmen's tools and techniques used locally before industrial age. Enquire locally for opening times.

Turquant
Musée de l'Outil
Moulin de la Herpinière (south of Turquant), 8km east of Saumur on south bank of Loire on D947.
Tel: (41)51 75 22 or 50 53 85
Restored fifteenth-century mill where statuary, paintings, tapestries, hand-painted wallpapers are made.
Open daily Easter to end September; closed Monday except July and August.

SARTHE
Beaumont-Pied-de-Boeuf
Costume Museum
8km north of Château-du-Loir on D73A.
Tel: (43)44 29 83
Open daily mid-July to end August and Sunday afternoon May to September.

La Flèche
Prytanée National Militaire

One-time Jesuit college, now preparatory
school for military colleges.
Open daily during summer holidays.

Chapelle Notre Dame des Vertus
Open daily. Apply to Maison d'Enfants
next door to see over Romanesque
building with Renaissance wood-carvings.

Jupilles
North on D73A from Château-du-Loir to
Beaumont-Pied-de-Boeuf, right on D73
(12.5km).
Tel: (43)79 42 67
Exhibition of traditional woodcraft (in
heart of Forêt de Bercé, 13,750 acres).
Open afternoons daily except Monday,
mid-April to September.

Poncé-sur-le-Loir
Musée d'Ethnographie du Maine
Regional ethnographic museum in
château.
Open March to mid-November, daily
except Sunday morning.

Atelier de la Volonière
Exhibition and sale of work: leather,
painted silks, antiques, dolls, painted
furniture.
Open daily all year, afternoon only on
Sunday and public holidays.

Artisanant, Grès du Loir
Moulin de Paillard.
Craft centre: pottery workshops, wrought-
ironwork, woodwork, weaving, glass-
blowing, lampshade making, wicker work.
Exhibition and sales.
Open daily all year, afternoon only on
Sunday and public holidays.

Pringé
North-east on N23 from La Flèche for
5.5km, right at Clermont-Créans on D13
for 6km.
Fifteenth-century church with sixteenth-
century murals. Ask for key at last house
on right at north exit of village.

Solesmes
Abbaye St Pierre
3km outside Sablé-sur-Sarthe.
Tel: (43)95 03 08
Abbey church only open to public.
Famous Gregorian chant sung at Mass at
10am Sunday and 9.45am weekdays;
Vespers at 5pm.

ANNUAL EVENTS

Amboise (Indre-et-Loire)
July, historical drama at château.

Angers (Maine-et-Loire)
End of June to mid-July, Anjou Festival of
concerts, plays, ballet, exhibitions. (Many
similar events are held at this time
throughout Maine-et-Loire.)

Beaugency (Loiret)
June, drama Festival at château.

Blois (Loir-et-Cher)
Mid-June, *Floréal Blésois*, carnival,
regatta, drama, music.

Bourges (Cher)
May, *'La Vieille Ville en Fête'*, carnival.
May to October, audio-visual show, *'La
Cathédrale de Bourges et les Monuments du
Cher'*.

Bourgueil (Indre-et-Loire)
First Saturday in February, Wine Fair.

Châteauneuf-sur-Loire (Loiret)
Whit Sunday, Rhododendron Festival.

Chênehutte (Maine-et-Loire)
Around 1 May, Mushroom Fair.

Cheverny (Loir-et-Cher)
Mid-July to mid-August, torchlight meet
of hounds, and horn concerts by *Trompes
de Cheverny*.

Chinon (Indre-et-Loire)
First weekend in August, medieval market
held in period costume, tasting of old
recipes, medieval trades, juggling, dancing,
singing.

Cunault (Maine-et-Loire)
Six Sundays a year between April and
September, *Les Dimanches animées de
Cunault*, market in village square featuring
crafts and local produce, circus, street
bands, folk groups, jugglers, refreshments.

Doué-la-Fontaine (Maine-et-Loire)
Mid-July, *Floralies de la Rose,*
International Rose Festival held in *Arène*
(old quarry with stepped seats).

Gien (Loiret)
Mid-August, every other (odd) year,

Historical Festival, drama shows and parades.

Jargeau (Loiret)
Mid-October, *Foire aux Chats* (or *châtaignes*), Chestnut Fair.

Langeais (Indre-et-Loire)
Late July to early August, International Music Festivals at Domaine de Vernou.
Tel: (47)96 80 59

Loches (Indre-et-Loire)
Mid-July, peasant market.

Menetou-Salon (Cher)
Mid-May, *Frairie des Brangers*, festival reconstructing past of village.
Tel: (48) 24 14 95

La Ménitré (Maine-et-Loire)
Third Sunday in July. Local folklore groups, displays of ancient costumes and headdresses.
24 December, *Messe des Naulets* in church. Local folklore groups sing Christmas carols in patois, dressed in old regional costume.

Meung-sur-Loire (Loiret)
9 June and 8 September, organ concerts at Collégiale St Liphard.
Tel: (38)44 32 58 or 44 43 94

Molineuf (Loir-et-Cher)
15 August, Bric-à-brac Fair.

Montoire-sur-le-Loir (Loir-et-Cher)
Mid-August, World Folklore Festival each evening, street processions, concerts.
Tel: (54)85 03 91 or 85 02 82

Olivet (Loiret)
Second week in June, water-sports festival on river Loiret.

Orléans (Loiret)
7 and 8 May, Joan of Arc Festival. Illumination of cathedral on 7 May; religious and secular ceremonies on 8 May.
Tel: (38)42 22 22
May to October, open air floral displays in Parc Floral de la Source.
Tel: (38)63 33 17

Sablé-sur-Sarthe (Sarthe)
Last Sunday in May, *Fête du Quéniau* (Children's Festival), costumes, dancing.

St Benoît (Loiret)
Easter Saturday, Vigil and Easter ceremony, and Gregorian chant at abbey. Christmas Eve, Gregorian chant at abbey.
Tel: (38)35 72 43

Ste Maure-de-Touraine (Indre-et-Loire)
June, Gastronomic Fair.

Saumur (Maine-et-Loire)
Second fortnight in July, *Grand Carrousel*, cavalry display by *Cadre Noir* and military tattoo.
Mid-September, equestrian fortnight.

Solesmes (Sarthe)
Holy Week, mass in abbey and Gregorian chant.
Christmas Eve, Midnight Mass.

Sully-sur-Loire (Loiret)
Whitsun week, orchestral concerts at château.
Friday and Saturday evenings in July, Music and drama festival at château.
Tel: (38)62 04 88
Last Sunday in October, meet of hounds and concert of hunting horns at château.

Tours (Indre-et-Loire)
Last weekend in June, first weekend in July, Music Festival of Touraine at Grange de Meslay, with international celebrities.
May, international choral singing.
May, flower pageant.
Early July, Choral Festival.
Last fortnight in July, Drama Festival.
Early August, Ballet Festival in garden of Musée des Beaux-Arts.

RIVERS AND LAKES

Many of the rivers and lakes are ready-made for aquatic sports, bathing or just sunbathing on natural sandy or shingly river- and lake-side beaches. Others have been made into well-equipped centres for sailing, water-skiing, windsurfing or fishing. A number of towns and villages have built swimming pools or sports complexes run by the municipality which are open to everyone.

Listed below are some of the lakes and riverside spots (in brackets is the name of the river) where there are beaches. All are safe. Elsewhere — and this applies particularly to the Loire — there can be a risk from deceptively strong currents (around 4km/h), eddies or sand spits which look firm enough but may be waterlogged quicksands.

Amboise (Loire), sailing; Ile d'Or leisure centre with swimming pool.
Angers (Maine), the Maine Lake, sailing, water-skiing.
Bléré (Cher), sailing.
Blois-les-Noëls, Lac du Loire (Loire), sailing, water-skiing and other leisure facilities.
Cerdon, Etang du Puits, sailing and extensive nautical facilities.
Château-la-Vallière, Etang du Val Joyeux.
Châteauneuf-sur-Loire (Loire).
Chinon (Vienne), sailing, canoeing, fishing.
Coëmont (Loir).
Combreux, Etang de la Vallée, all water sports, hire of boats and pedalos.
Gien (Loire).
Le Gué-du-Loir (Loir).
Ingrandes (Loire).
Langeais (Loire), sailing.
Loches (Indre), nautical centre with open-air and covered and heated swimming-pools.
Marçon, Lac des Varennes, canoeing, fishing, sailing, windsurfing.
Montsoreau (Loire), sailing, water-skiing.
Noyen-sur-Sarthe (Sarthe).
Orléans (Loire), beaches of Ile Arrault and Ile Charlemagne.
Orléans (Loiret), canoeing.
Parcé-sur-Sarthe (Sarthe).
Les Ponts-de-Cé (Loire).
Rillé, Lac de Pincemaille.
Saumur (Loire), sailing, water-skiing.
Le Thoureil (Loire), sailing, water-skiing.
Tours (Loire), sailing, canoeing.
Tours (Cher), lake and park of St Avertin, sailing, pedalos, swimming-pool, fishing.
Vaas (Loir).

RIVER CRUISES AND ADVENTURE HOLIDAYS

Angers: boat and barge excursions along river Layon. Cruises along rivers Sarthe, Mayenne, Loire in *Roi René I* and *Roi René II* with lunch on board. Houseboat hire (for day, weekend, week or longer) for whole Bassin de la Maine with 250km of waterways along Sarthe (twenty locks between Angers and Le Mans), Mayenne (twenty-five locks between Angers and

Laval), Oudon (three locks between Segré and Le Lion d'Angers); can include bicycle and tent hire; opportunities for white fish angling; eight boat-hire companies offer eighty boats of various types, based at Angers and six other centres listed below with *.
Information, booking at all centres at Maine Reservation, Maison de Tourisme, Place Kennedy, 49000 Angers.
Tel: (41)88 99 38

Beaugency: kayak and cycling holidays for two weeks for people between ages of 18 and 30 who are swimmers. Overnight accommodation in Youth Hostels and tents on certain dates in July and August. First week cycling: Beaugency to Châtillon-sur-Loire. Second week kayaking: Châtillon to Beaugency.
Information from Loisirs-Accueil-Loiret, 3 Rue de la Bretonnerie, 45000 Orléans.
Tel: (38)62 04 88
(Note: descent of Loire in canoe-kayak possible between Roanne and Ancenis, requiring skill and experience.)

Blois: boating and camping weekends under guidance of professional pilot. Flat-bottomed boats with cabin, emergency outboard motor. Planned picnic stops at islands in Loire.
Information from Loisirs-Accueil-Loiret-Cher, 11 Place du Château, 41000 Blois.
Tel: (54)78 55 50

Blois, Tours or Angers: cruises in *gabarre*, traditional Loire barge carrying twelve passengers, between Blois and Tours, or Tours and Angers during season.
Enquire at Tourist Office at Blois, Tours, Angers.

Briare: motorised rubber dinghy holidays, up- or down-stream of Loire. Inflatable dinghies of 'Bombard Commando' type, three to five passengers. Hire by day, weekend, week; camping equipment provided.
Information from Loisirs-Accueil-Loiret, 3 Rue de la Bretonnerie, 45000 Orléans.
Tel: (38)62 04 88

***Châteauneuf-sur-Sarthe**: boat-hire centre on river Sarthe. Cruises on *Roi René I* or *Roi René II*, 15 June to 15 September.

Châtillon-sur-Loire: hire of cabin cruisers for six, for weekends or week.
Reservation at Loisirs-Accueil-Loiret, 3 Rue de la Bretonnerie, 45000 Orléans.
Tel: (38)62 04 88

*Chenillé-Changé: boat-hire centre on river Mayenne.

*Grez-Neuville: boat-hire centre on river Mayenne.

*Malicorne-sur-Sarthe: boat-hire centre.

*Noyen-sur-Sarthe: boat-hire centre.

Olivet: rowing-punts for hire at establishments in Rue Albert Berbier.

*Sablé-sur-Sarthe: boat-hire centre. Also cruises of 110 mins by the *Sablésien* (85 passengers) with commentary along river Sarthe; Friday and Saturday at 4.45pm between end June and mid-August. Tel: (43)95 93 13

ANGLING

Fast-running tributaries of the Loire (like the Loire itself well upstream in its more mountainous course) are rated First Category with trout predominating. Open season from third Saturday in February to last Monday in September.

In the Loire Valley region, the Loire and slow-running tributaries are Second Category with coarse fish forming the majority. Open season from mid-June to mid-April.

At many places fishing is authorised. Permits issued by the *département* are for a whole year. Shops selling fishing tackle are sometimes able to issue permits for a fee. At some privately owned lakes, day permits are provided against payment.

Fish likely to be met with in the rivers: bream, bullhead, carp, grey mullet (which work their way upstream from the Atlantic), perch, pike, roach, shad, trout and zander.

WALKING

Footpaths abound for those who want to take short walks. Long-distance walks along marked paths (*Sentiers de grande randonnée*) are shown by broken lines on Michelin maps which give also route numbers, eg GR3 or GR46. A number of these pass through the Loire Valley. You can follow the north bank of the Loire from Orléans to Blois. Others criss-cross Sologne (one route goes from Gien to

Chambord), Indre Valley, Vendômois, through Orléans Forest, the largest in France.

Most local tourist offices can supply information and sketch maps of interesting paths in the vicinity. For much more detailed guidance, it is wise to join the nation-wide organisation, *Comité National des Sentiers de Grande Randonnée,* 92 Rue de Clignancourt, 75883 Paris. Tel: (1)259 60 40

Ask at tourist offices for information about nature trails or guides who give instruction about local flora and fauna.

RIDING

Riding schools for all grades of proficiency and pony-trekking are everywhere available. Riding holidays of varying lengths include visits to châteaux; accommodation may be at the school or at farms. Departmental *Loisirs-Accueil* offices will supply details and effect bookings.

GYPSY CARAVAN HOLIDAYS

A popular form of holidaymaking is the hire of horse-drawn caravans for weekends, a week or fortnight. Caravans vary in size and hold from four to ten people. Apply to *Loisirs-Accueil* offices. In Sarthe: Locattelage, La Petite Chauvière, Laigne-en-Belin, 72520 St Gervais-en-Belin. Tel: (43)21 51 44

EQUESTRIAN DISPLAY

Domaine de Fontiville, Veigné (Indre-et-Loire), tel: (47)26 03 94. South from Tours on N10 for 8km, left at Les Gués-de-Veigné on D50; follow signposts after 1.3km. Display of eighteenth-century French riding by *Académie Equestre de Touraine* on Saturday at 9pm from beginning of May to late September, but closed during last fortnight in August.

CYCLING

Visitors arriving by train can hire bicycles

at all major railway stations. Many cycle shops in towns and villages hire out bicycles for fixed periods. Some of them arrange itineraries for individuals and groups, particularly for young people between the ages of 18 and 30. These can be for a week or two weeks, with fixed departure dates in July, August and September, with Youth Hostel or tent accommodation. Some itineraries visit châteaux and vineyards. Tourist offices can supply details.

GOLF

Angers: Golf de St Jean-des-Mauvrets, 9 holes. Tel: (41)91 92 15. 8km south-east of Angers.

Le Ferté-St Aubin: 18 holes. 5km north-west of town.

Orléans: Loire Valley Golf Club at Donnery, 9 holes. Tel: (38)59 20 48. 8km east of Orléans. Instruction at all levels, weekend or four-day courses. Hotel accommodation if required.

Sully-sur-Loire: Domaine de Lousseau, Viglain, 18 holes. 4km west of Sully. Four-day courses, May to October, for novices to advanced players. Accommodation available. Closed Tuesday.

Tours: Touraine Golf Club, Domaine de la Touche, Ballan-Miré, 18 holes. Tel: (47)53 20 28. 10km south-west of Tours. Open daily except Tuesday. Offers daily rates to visitors holding membership card from another club. Golfing holidays in conjunction with Château-Hôtel d'Artigny, Montbazon. Tel: (47)26 24 24.

WILDLIFE, ZOOS AND GARDENS

Angers (Maine-et-Loire)
Arboretum de la Maulévrie
Jardin des Plantes, off Boulevard Carnot. Exotic trees.

Forêt de Bercé (Sarthe)
Guided visits round Futaie des Clos by official of National Forestry Office, daily except Tuesday, at 9.30am and 3pm. Point of departure, Chêne Boppe parking area east of Jupilles.

Châteauneuf-sur-Loire (Loiret)
Arboretum du Château
Tel: (38)58 41 18
Chiefly giant rhododendrons in grounds of château. Open daily all year.

Doué-la-Fontaine (Maine-et-Loire)
Zoo des Minières
300 animals in disused quarries. Open all year.

La Flèche (Sarthe)
Parc Zoologique de Tertre Rouge
Tel: (43)94 04 55
5km south-east on D104. Open all day all year. Wide variety of wild animals in 18 acres of forest; small natural history museum with dioramas of regional fauna.

Le Lion-d'Angers (Maine-et-Loire)
Haras national (National Stud)
Château Isle-Briand.
Open all year. Visit to saddle-room, smithy, riding-school, stables of different breeds of horses including retired race-horses at stud. Displays of harnesses and stallions between October and February at 2.30pm on first Wednesday of each month.

La Ferté-St Aubin (Loiret),
Domaine Solognot du Ciran
6km east of town, left at Les Quatre Routes on D108, left after 1km.
Tel: (38)65 90 93
Sologne wildlife and walks through characteristic Sologne countryside (1-2 hours; boots advised). Open daily all year. Advance notice required for groups, and those wanting guided tours. Small museum of Sologne bygones in château.

Orléans-la-Source (Loiret)
Parc Floral at Olivet
Tel: (38)63 33 17
Open afternoons, January to March and mid-November to December; open daily April to mid-November. Pamphlets in English. Floral park and animals; greenhouse-restaurant. Miniature train (25 mins) in Floral Park runs afternoons only on Wednesday, Friday, Saturday, April; afternoons daily except Thursday, May to September; afternoons only, Wednesday, Friday, Saturday, October.

Richelieu (Indre-et-Loire)
Gardens of château
Open daily all year. 45 hectacres of formal grounds belonging to University of Paris.

St Aignan-sur-Cher (Loir-et-Cher)
Parc Ornithologique de Beauval
4km south of St Aignan on D675.
Tel: (54)75 05 56
Bird sanctuary concentrating on
endangered species. Open daily to nightfall
all year.

St Denis-de-l'Hôtel (Loiret)
Parc Floral Henri Coulland
Tel: (38)59 02 24
Flower gardens. Open daily all year.

Valençay (Indre)
Zoo et Parc du Château
Tel: (54)00 10 66
Zoo in grounds of château. Open daily
mid-March to mid-September; all day
Friday and Saturday, January to mid-
March.

Verneuil-sur-Indre (Indre)
Floral gardens run by horticultural college
in grounds of château. Open between June
and October.

Villandry (Indre-et-Loire)
Jardin du Château
Tel: (47)50 02 09
Visit of formal gardens only (45 mins).
Open daily all year.

STEAM RAILWAYS

Marcilly-sur-Maulne (Indre-et-Loire)
West of Château-la-Vallière, *Train à
vapeur.*
Tel: (47)24 07 95 or 24 04 46
Narrow-gauge railway, 2km track, and
collection of engines, etc. Open Sunday
afternoon, May to mid-September for trip
with old steam locomotive (or sometimes
diesel) on certain dates. Train available to
groups by previous arrangement, Monday
to Saturday.

Chinon — Richelieu — Chinon (Indre-et-
Loire)
Trains à vapeur de Touraine.
Steam train journeys, single or return, on
Saturday and Sunday from early May to
mid-September, using early twentieth-
century rolling-stock. Leisurely trip
through fields, vineyards, woodlands with
wayside halts for local wine and cheese
tasting. Information at Chinon railway
station, SNCF (Tel: (47)58 12 97) or Tours
station, SNCF (Tel: (47)61 46 46).

**Salbris — Buzançais; Romorantin-
Lanthenay — Salbris — Romorantin-
Lanthenay** (Loir-et-Cher and Indre)
Special steam train excursions. Details
from Salbris Syndicat d'Initiative,
Tel: (54)83 06 54.

FROM THE AIR

Short trips by light aircraft are available
from the following airfields. One or two
also use helicopters.

Aéro-Club de Touraine, Tours-Sorigny,
37250 Montbazon.
Tel: (47)26 01 14
Circuit of châteaux.

Les Ailes Tourangelles, Aérodrome
d'Amboise-Dierre.

Aéro-Club de Sologne, 4 Rue des Trois-
Rois, 41200 Romorantin-Lanthenay.
Tel: (54)76 04 48

Aérodrome du Breuil, Villefrancoeur,
41000 Blois.
Tel: (54)79 17 68

Aérodrome Orléans-Saran.
Tel: (38)87 43 36
Choice of three twenty-minute circuits;
aircraft carry five passengers.

Les Montgolfières de France, Le Paradis,
La Croix-en-Touraine, 37150 Bléré.
Hot air balloon flights in fine weather.

TASTING WINE

In all wine producing areas are *caves*
(cellars) which invite *dégustation* (tasting).
They range from large co-operatives selling
local table wine to small private *caves*
which are outlets for the produce of a
single vineyard. Wine can be bought in
single bottles or in bulk. Most places do
not charge for entrance and you can
usually go in unannounced during the
opening times of the establishment. A few
are visited by previous arrangement only.

Cher

Menetou-Salon, Caves Gilbert, Les Faucards.
Tel: (48)64 80 77

Preuilly, Cave de l'Union Viticole, Le Carroir.
Tel: (48)51 30 78

Quincy, Cave de l'Union Viticole.
Tel: (48)51 31 17

Indre-et-Loire

Amboise, Cave Denay, La Briquetterie.
Tel: (47)57 11 53

Amboise, Cave Girault-Artois, 7 Quai des Violettes.
Tel: (47)57 07 71

Bourgueil, Cave Touristique de la Dive-Bouteille, Chevrette.
Tel: (47)97 72 01

Chançay, Cave Vigneau-Chevreau, 4 Rue de Clos Baguelin.
Tel: (47)52 93 22

Chargé, Cave Mangeant, La Graverie, Rue du Général de Gaulle.
Tel: (47)57 09 75

Chinon, Musée du Vin, Rue du Dr Gendron.

Chinon, Cave Plouzeau, 94 Rue Haute St Maurice.
Tel: (47)93 16 34

Ligré, Cave Manzagol, La Noblaie.
Tel: (47)93 10 96

Limeray, Cave Dutertre, 20-21 Rue d'Enfer.
Tel: (47)30 10 69

Montlouis-sur-Loire, Cave Coopérative des Producteurs de Vins de Montlouis, 2 Route de St Aignan.
Tel: (47)50 80 98

Montlouis-sur-Loire, Cave Touristique de Montlouis, Place Courtemanche.
Tel: (47)50 82 26

Tours, Maison des Vins de Touraine, 19 Square Prosper Mérimée.
Tel: (47)05 40 01

Vouvray, Cave Coopérative des Producteurs des Grands Vins de Vouvray, Vallée Coquette.
Tel: (47)52 75 02

Vouvray, Cave des Viticulteurs du Vouvray, Château de Vaudenuits.
Tel: (47)52 60 20

Vouvray, Cave Daniel Jarry, La Caillerie, Route de la Vallée Coquette.
Tel: (47)52 78 75

Vouvray, Cave de la Bonne Dame, wine fair early January and 15 August.

Loir-et-Cher

Cellettes, Cave Dorléans, Domaine de la Gaudronnière.
Tel: (54)44 20 41

Chémery, Cave de la Grande Brosse.
Tel: (54)71 81 03

Chissay-en-Touraine, Distillerie 'Fraise d'Or', 62 Route de Tours.
Tel: (54)32 32 05
Manufacture of strawberry liqueur.

Mesland, Caves Brosillon, Domaine de Lusqueneau.
Tel: (54)79 78 23

Montrichard, Caves Montmousseau, 71 Rue de Vierzon.
Tel: (54)32 07 04

Montrichard, Cave de Champagnisation.
Seur, Cave A Coutoux, 5 Chemin des Murs.
Tel: (54)44 04 58

Loiret

Beaulieu-sur-Loire, Cave de M. Guerot, 'L'Étang'.
Tel: (38)35 81 58

Mareau-aux-Prés, Cave Coopérative, 550 Route des Muids.
Tel: (38)45 61 08

Olivet, Covifruit, 613 Rue du Pressoir-Tonneau.
Tel: (38)63 40 20

Maine-et-Loire

Angers, Distillerie Cointreau, St Barthélémy d'Anjou.
Tel: (41)41 25 21

Angers, Maison du Vin.
Tel: (41)88 81 13

Angers, Distillerie Giffard.
Tel: (41) 34 52 23

Liré, Cave Du Bellay.
Tel: (41)83 03 26

Louresse-Rochemenier, Cave et Musée.
Tel: (41)59 13 13

St Cyr-en-Bourg, Cave Coopérative des Vignerons de Saumur.
Tel: (41)51 61 09

St Hilaire-St Florent, Caves Ackerman-Laurence.
Tel: (41)50 25 33
Of note because John Ackerman came to Saumur in 1811 to introduce the *méthode champenoise* to Saumur wines.

St Hilaire-St Florent, Caves Bouvet-Ladubay.
Tel: (41)50 16 43

St Hilaire-St Florent, Cave de Neuville.
Tel: (41)50 16 43

St Hilaire-St Florent, Cave Veuve Amiot.
Tel: (41)50 25 24

Saumur, Cave Gratien-Meyer.
Tel: (41)51 04 54

Saumur, Maison du Vin.
Tel: (41)51 16 40
Next to Office de Tourisme, 25 Rue Beaurepaire.

Sarthe
Chahaignes, Cave Mr Bouin, Société La Malvoyère.
Tel: (43)44 46 19

La Chartre-sur-le-Loir, Cave Mr Gigou.
Tel: (43)44 48 72

La Chartre-sur-le-Loir, Cave Mr Barbier.
Tel: (43)44 40 82

L'Homme, Cave Mr Pinon, 'Les Tuffières'.
Tel: (43)85 30 56

L'Homme, Cave Mr Boutard, 'La Varenne'.
Tel: (43)44 43 63

L'Homme, Cave Mr Branjonneau, 'Les Jasnières'.
Tel: (43)79 03 53

L'Homme, Cave Mr Cartereau, 'Bordebeurre'.
Tel: (43)44 48 66

Marçon, Cave Mr Cronier, 'Le Bourg'.
Tel: (43)44 13 20

Vouvray-sur-Loir, Cave Municipale, Mairie.
Tel: (43)44 14 15

Town Hotels

The hotels in this list are in the larger towns, and are conveniently placed for local sightseeing. Following the hotel's name is its postal address and telephone number. Only those establishments which have private garage or parking facilities are included, as many visitors do not want to leave their cars overnight in public parking places or in the streets.

Amboise (Indre-et-Loire)
Hôtel Chanteloup, Route de Bléré, 37400 Amboise. 25 rooms (room and breakfast only).
Tel: (47)57 10 90

Novotel, Route de Chenonceaux, 37400 Amboise. 82 rooms.
Tel: (47)57 42 07

Angers (Maine-et-Loire)
Hôtel Anjou et Restaurant Salamandre, 1 Boulevard Maréchal Foch, 49000 Angers. 51 rooms.
Tel: (41) 88 24 82

Hôtel Croix de Guerre, 23 Rue Château Gontier, 49000 Angers. 28 rooms (room and breakfast only).
Tel: (41)88 66 59

Hôtel St Jacques, 83 Rue St Jacques, 49000 Angers. 19 rooms.
Tel: (41)48 51 05

Beaugency (Loiret)
Hôtel l'Abbaye, Quai Abbaye, 45190 Beaugency. 13 rooms and 5 apartments.
Tel: (38)44 67 35

Ecu de Bretagne, Place Martroi, 45190 Beaugency. 26 rooms.
Tel: (38)44 67 60

Blois (Loir-et-Cher)
Hôtel du Grand Cerf, 40 Avenue Wilson, 41000 Blois. 14 rooms.
Tel: (54)78 02 16

Hôtel Monarque, 61 Rue Porte Chartraine, 41000 Blois. 22 rooms.
Tel: (54)78 02 35.

Bourges (Cher)
Hôtel des Étrangers, 6 Rue Cambournac, 18000 Bourges. 22 rooms (room and breakfast only).
Tel: (48)24 01 15

Hôtel Olympia, 66 Avenue Orléans, 18000 Bourges. 42 rooms (room and breakfast only).
Tel: (48)70 49 84

Châteauneuf-sur-Loire (Loiret)
La Capitainerie, Grande-Rue, 45110
Châteauneuf-sur-Loire. 14 rooms.
Tel: (38)58 42 16

Nouvel Hôtel du Loiret, Place Aristide
Briand, 45110 Châteauneuf-sur-Loire. 20
rooms.
Tel: (38)58 42 28

Château-Renault (Indre-et-Loire)
Hôtel Lion d'Or, 166 Rue République,
37110 Château-Renault. 10 rooms.
Tel: (47)56 96 50

Chinon (Indre-et-Loire)
Hôtel Diderot, 7 Rue Diderot, 37500
Chinon. 20 rooms (room and breakfast
only).
Tel: (47)93 18 87

La Ferté-St Aubin (Loiret)
Hôtel Perron, Rue Général Leclerc, 45240
La Ferté-St Aubin. 30 rooms.
Tel: (38)76 53 36

La Flèche (Sarthe)
Hôtel Quatre Vents, 11 Rue Marché-au-
Blé, 72200 La Flèche. 15 rooms (room and
breakfast only).
Tel: (43)94 00 61

Gien (Loiret)
Hôtel Rivage, 1 Quai Nice, 45500 Gien. 29
rooms.
Tel: (38)67 20 53

Loches (Indre-et-Loire)
Hôtel France, 6 Rue Picois, 37600 Loches.
22 rooms.
Tel: (47)59 00 32

Le Lude (Sarthe)
Hôtel Maine, 24 Avenue Saumur, 72800 Le
Lude. 24 rooms.
Tel: (43)94 60 54

Mehun-sur-Yèvre (Cher)
Hôtel Croix-Blanche, 164 Rue Jeanne
d'Arc, 18500 Mehun-sur-Yèvre. 20 rooms.
Tel: (48)57 30 01

Meung-sur-Loire (Loiret)
Auberge St Jacques, Rue Général de
Gaulle, 45130 Meung-sur-Loire. 12 rooms.
Tel: (38)44 30 39

Montoire-sur-le-Loir (Loir-et-Cher)
Hôtel Cheval Rouge, Place Foch, 41800
Montoire. 17 rooms.
Tel: (54)85 07 05

Olivet (Loiret)
Frantel Reine Blanche, 635 Rue Reine-
Blanche, 45160 Olivet. 65 rooms.
Tel: (38)66 40 51

Hôtel les Quatre Saisons, 351 Rue Reine-
Blanche, 45160 Olivet. 10 rooms.
Tel: (38)66 14 30

Hôtel Le Rivage, 638, Rue Reine-Blanche,
45160 Olivet. 21 rooms.
Tel: (38)66 02 93

Orléans (Loiret)
Hôtel St Aignan, 3 Place Gambetta, 45000
Orléans. 27 rooms (room and breakfast
only).
Tel: (38)53 15 35

Hôtel St Jean, 19 Rue Porte St Jean, 45000
Orléans. 27 rooms (room and breakfast
only).
Tel: (38)53 63 32

Sofitel, 44 Quai Barentin, 45000 Orléans.
108 rooms.
Tel: (38)62 17 39

Romorantin-Lanthenay (Loir-et-Cher)
Hôtel Le Colombier, 10 Place Vieux-
Marché, 41200 Romorantin-Lanthenay. 10
rooms.
Tel: (54)76 12 76

Grand Hôtel du Lion d'Or, 69 Rue
Clemenceau, 41200 Romorantin-
Lanthenay. 8 rooms.
Tel: (54)76 00 28

Salbris (Loir-et-Cher)
Hôtel du Parc, 10 Avenue Orléans, 41300
Salbris. 29 rooms.
Tel: (54)97 18 53

La Sauldraie, 41300 Salbris. 13 rooms.
Tel: (54)97 17 76

Saumur (Maine-et-Loire)
Hôtel Croix Verte, 49 Rue de Rouen,
49400 Saumur. 18 rooms.
Tel: (41)67 39 31

Hôtel Londres, 48 Rue d'Orléans, 49400
Saumur. 26 rooms (room and breakfast

only).
Tel: (41)51 23 98

Sully-sur-Loire (Loiret)
Hôtel Pont de Sologne, Rue Porte de
Sologne, 45600 Sully. 25 rooms.
Tel: (38)36 26 34

Hôtel Poste, Rue Faubourg St Germain,
45600 Sully. 27 rooms.
Tel: (38)36 26 22

Tours (Indre-et-Loire)
Hôtel Criden, 65 Boulevard Heurteloup,
37000 Tours. 33 rooms (room and
breakfast only).
Tel: (47)20 81 14

Hôtel Cygne, 6 Rue Cygne, 37000 Tours.
20 rooms (room and breakfast only).
Tel: (47)66 66 41

Hôtel Méridien, 292 Avenue Grammont,
37000 Tours. 119 rooms and 6 apartments.
Tel: (47)28 00 80

Vendôme (Loir-et-Cher)
Hôtel Moderne, 41100 Vendôme (facing
railway station). 16 rooms.
Tel: (54)77 21 15

Hôtel Vendôme, 15 Faubourg Chartrain,
41100 Vendôme. 35 rooms.
Tel: (54)77 02 88

Vierzon (Cher)
Hôtel Continental, Route de Paris, 18100
Vierzon. 36 rooms.
Tel: (48)75 35 22

SOME RURAL HOTELS

This is a selection of country hotels, some
set deep in the countryside, others sited in
villages or small townships. They avoid the
hurly-burly often associated with hotels in
larger towns, and the starchy pretensions
of hotels of great renown. Most are small
enough for the owner's personality to
stamp itself on the atmosphere of the
place. All the hotels are personal
recommendations (though not necessarily
my own). Each should be able to provide
the visitor with an agreeable recollection of
his stay. Comfort, consideration, enjoyable
food, pleasant surroundings and views, a
sense of relaxation, an attractive character
are some of the qualities of these hotels
(though you must not expect to find them
all in any one of them). All are modestly
priced; they give value in a number of
particulars without making you feel that
you are having to pay a stiff price for the
privilege.

Baugé (Maine-et-Loire)
Hôtel Boule d'Or, 4 Rue Cygne, 49150
Baugé. 14 rooms.
Tel: (41)89 82 12

Brinon-sur-Sauldre (Cher)
La Solognote, 18410 Argent-sur-Sauldre.
10 rooms.
Tel: (48)58 50 29

Candé-sur-Beuvron (Loir-et-Cher)
Hôtel Lion d'Or, 41120 Les Montils. 10
rooms.
Tel: (54)44 06 66

La Chartre-sur-le-Loir (Sarthe)
Hôtel de France, 72340 La Chartre. 32
rooms in annexe.
Tel: (43)44 40 16

Châteauneuf-sur-Sarthe (Maine-et-Loire)
Hôtel Sarthe, 49330 Châteauneuf. 7
rooms.
Tel: (41)42 11 30

Cour-Cheverny (Loir-et-Cher)
Hôtel Les Trois Marchands, 41700
Contres. 43 rooms.
Tel: (54)79 96 44

Gennes (Maine-et-Loire)
Hostellerie de la Loire, 49350 Gennes. 11
rooms.
Tel: (41)51 81 03

Lanthenay (Loir-et-Cher)
Hôtel Le Lanthenay, Place de l'Eglise,
41200 Romorantin-Lanthenay. 14 rooms.
Tel: (54)76 09 19

Luché-Pringé (Sarthe)
Auberge du Port des Roches, Port des
Roches, 72800 Le Lude. 15 rooms.
Tel: (43)94 43 23

Matheflon (Maine-et-Loire)
Hostellerie St Jacques, 49140 Seiches-sur-
le-Loir. 10 rooms.
Tel: (41)80 00 30

Montbazon (Indre-et-Loire)
Auberge Moulin Fleuri, 37250
Montbazon. 10 rooms.
Tel: (47)26 01 12

Montreuil-Bellay (Maine-et-Loire)
Hôtel Splendid et Relais du Bellay, Rue Dr
Gaudrez, 49260 Montreuil-Bellay. 15
rooms and 20 in annexe.
Tel: (41)52 30 21

Montsoreau (Maine-et-Loire)
Hôtel Bussy et Diane de Méridor, 49730
Montsoreau. 19 rooms.
Tel: (41)51 70 18

Nouan-le-Fuzelier (Loir-et-Cher)
Les Charmilles, 41600 Lamotte-Beuvron.
14 rooms (room and breakfast only).
Tel: (54)88 73 55

Moulin de Villiers, 41600 Lamotte-
Beuvron. 20 rooms.
Tel: (54)88 72 27

Onzain (Loir-et-Cher)
Hôtel Pont d'Ouchet, Grande Rue, 41150
Onzain. 10 rooms.
Tel: (54)20 70 33

Château des Tertres, 41150, Onzain. 14
rooms (room and breakfast only).
Tel: (54)20 83 88

Oucques (Loir-et-Cher)
Hôtel Commerce, 41290 Oucques. 7
rooms.
Tel: (54)23 20 41

Les Rosiers (Maine-et-Loire)
Hôtel Val de Loire, Place de l'Eglise, 49350
Gennes. 11 rooms.
Tel: (41)51 80 30

Jeanne de Laval, Route Nationale, 49350
Gennes. 7 rooms and 8 in annexe Ducs
d'Anjou.
Tel: (41)51 80 17

St Aignan (Loir-et-Cher)
Grand Hôtel St Aignan, 41110 St Aignan.
23 rooms.
Tel: (54)75 18 04

St Dyé-sur-Loire (Loir-et-Cher)
Manoir Bel Air, 41500 Mer. 30 rooms.
Tel: (54)81 60 10

St Florent-le-Vieil (Maine-et-Loire)
Hostellerie de la Gabelle, 49410 St Florent-
le-Vieil. 17 rooms.
Tel: (41)78 50 19

Ste Montaine (Cher)
Hôtel Le Cheval Blanc, 18700 Aubigny-
sur-Nère. 18 rooms.
Tel: (48)58 06 92

St Martin-d'Auxigny (Cher)
Hôtel St Georges, La Pipière, 18110 St
Martin-d'Auxigny. 10 rooms.
Tel: (48)64 50 14

Vernous-sur-Brenne (Indre-et-Loire)
Hostellerie Perce-Neige, Rue Anatole
France, 37210 Vouvray. 8 rooms.
Tel: (47)52 10 04

Vierzon (Cher)
Hôtel Le Sologne, Route de Châteauroux,
18100 Vierzon. 24 rooms (room and
breakfast only).
Tel: (48)75 15 20

Villandry (Indre-et-Loire)
Hôtel Cheval Rouge, 37510 Joué-lès-
Tours. 20 rooms.
Tel: (47)50 02 07

BIBLIOGRAPHY

Atterbury, Paul, *Guide to the Loire Region.*
(Nicholson, 1985)
The Châteaux of the Loire. (Michelin Green
Guide, current edition)
Delpal, Jacques-Louis, *Loire Valley.*
(Automobile Association, 1985)
Dunlop, Ian, *Châteaux of the Loire.*
(Hamish Hamilton, 1969)
Grigson, Geoffrey, *Notes from an Odd
Country.* (Macmillan, 1970)
Hansmann, Wilfred, *DuMont Guide: The*

Loire, translated by Russell Stockman. (Webb & Bower, 1985)

Jennet, Seán, *The Loire.* (Batsford, 1975)

Layton, T.A., *Wines and Châteaux of the Loire.* (Cassell, 1967)

Loire Valley, Normandy, Brittany. (Ernest Benn Blue Guide, 1978)

Martin-Demézel, Jean, *The Loire Valley and its Treasures.* (George Allen & Unwin, 1969)

Melchior-Bonnet, Sabine, *Châteaux of the Loire,* translated by Angela Armstrong. (Paris: Librairie Larousse, 1984)

Myhill, Henry, *The Loire Valley.* (Faber & Faber, 1978)

Rowe, Vivian, *The Loire.* (Eyre & Spottiswoode, 1969)

Wade, Richard, *Companion Guide to the Loire.* (Collins, 1984)

Wylie, Laurence, *Chanzeaux: A Village in Anjou.* (Cambridge, Mass: Harvard University Press, 1966)

Index